THE **ULTIMATE GUIDE** TO
MINIGAMES & SERVERS

T0164280

This book is available in quantity at special discounts for your group or organization. For further information, contact:

Triumph Books LLC
814 North Franklin Street
Chicago, Illinois 60610
Phone: (312) 337-0747
www.triumphbooks.com

Printed in U.S.A.
ISBN: 978-1-62937-233-4

Content packaged by Mojo Media, Inc.
Joe Funk: Editor
Jason Hinman: Creative Director
Trevor Talley: Writer

Contents

Screenshot text:
Welcome to Turbo Kart Racers!
W to accelerate
S to ...
A and ... to st...
Jump to use your horn

TURBO KART RACE
Map: Canyon
Players: 11/12

Starting in 5s

Server: mini39M

www.hypixel.net

ing you to mini39M!
neuronaut has joined (9/12)!
elMasterX has joined (10/12)!
erDude222 has joined (11/12)!
game starts in 10 seconds!
game starts in 5 seconds!

Introduction

Ah, minigames! Those saviors of Minecraft that take our vanilla-jaded minds and turn them onto something new and awesome that makes Minecraft feel like a whole new game.

Since even the earliest days of Minecraft, creative folks out there have been taking the rules of this blocky building game and have made entirely new games out of it! These are what we mean when we use the term minigame, a term that essentially just means a new way to play Minecraft with everything from new rules to new items, and, always, other players to play along with you.

The many, many kinds of minigames people have come up with inside of Minecraft is frankly amazing, and in fact some of them are so much fun that many players now do nothing but play them instead of the regular game!

This has especially become the norm for online Minecraft servers on the PC edition of the game, where minigame playing has turned into an entire culture of its own.

Of course, we do love vanilla Minecraft, but after countless dozens of hours, even the world's best game can get a little old hat. Lucky for us Crafters, Minecraft is set up so that it is ideal for intrepid creators around the world to modify and turn into all sorts of other games.

That's what this book is all about. What games are out there, what games are most popular, how to play 'em and where to find 'em! We'll explain each game, tell you how to play it, give you the basic strategies that will start to get you wins in no time, and even throw in a handful of pro tips to really amp up your skills!

Whether you're an oldschool Crafter looking to spice up your game, or whether you're a new Minecrafter looking to see what all this fuss about online Minecraft is about, or whether you're already on Minecraft servers and want to take your minigame playing to the next level, this is the book for you.

Game on, Crafters!

The Many Wondrous Styles of Minigames

Before we jump into the nitty gritty of this thing and get you some game tips, let's break down the general types of games in this book.

There are about as many types of minigames in existence as there are plug-in creators and Redstone engineers that create them. There are always new variations and entirely new styles of minigames out there, but since Minecraft has been around for a while, a few genres have become established and most minigames new and old fall into them.

These, young Crafters, are the genres we're going to get you familiar with in this book, and will having you beating people at all over the Internet in no time.

SURVIVAL-BASED

Minecraft's about two things in the regular version of the game: survival and building. Learning how to do these two things is learning how to Minecraft, and people really pride themselves on their abilities in these departments.

Thus, when people set out to make minigames that took the regular game of Minecraft and made it competitive, one of the first things people did was to make a bunch of Survival-Based Minecraft minigames to pit their hard-won skills against those of their friends and the rest of the Internet.

These games will test your ability to simply stay alive and thrive in Minecraft, forcing you to mine for resources, hunt mobs, craft items, and even enchant a thing or two in some cases. On top of that, almost all Survival-Based minigames also require you to vanquish other players to win.

These are some hard minigames, but they're also highly rewarding and very beloved by the community.

PARKOUR

Parkour is different from just about every other minigame in this book, because it's not really about surviving, fighting, or building, but instead just plain jumping! Parkour is the art of jumping from block to block, and it's gone from being an obscure part of the online game to a bona fide phenomenon that you can find on almost every single server.

Parkour feels like an easier, less-intimidating minigame on the surface: you just jump from spot to spot, and when you fall down no alarms go off or "You Lose" signs flash or anything (usually, there are some competitive Parkour servers where things are a little more formalized). You just go back to the first block and start again, and you can go as slow as you want.

However, thinking of Parkour as easy is a mistake. This is one of the most tricky minigames in existence; one that takes years of practice and an incredible sense of timing and spatial recognition to get truly good at.

You can try, and we'll give you some tips, but beware Crafters: Parkour is some hardcore Minecraft minigamin'.

PLAYER VS. PLAYER

Person on person combat is the focus of most video games out there, and where regular, single-player Minecraft doesn't have it very often (except when you're being funny and slap your friend), online Minecraft has taken Player vs. Player (or PVP) combat and turned it into an art form.

There are literally hundreds of different variations on PVP minigames online today, from the easy and cute Spleef to the complex and difficult games like Warlords and Annihilation.

If you can think of it, from gun-based shootouts to Bow-only combat, people have probably made a formal, score-keeping minigame out of it and play it like crazy on some server or another. In this book, we've collected the best of the best, as well as the games that are most popular online right now. We'll walk you through how they work and how to get better at them, so that next time you log in, you'll find nobody on the server who can match your skills in combat.

SKYBLOCK AND SKYBLOCK VARIANTS

While a lot of games in this book have similarities to other video games you might play (such as the PVP games to first-person shooters), Skyblock is a style of minigame that's pretty much entirely unique to Minecraft. It involves surviving and performing challenges by crafting, but doing so while high up in the air on a teeny little block of land.

Skyblock takes a whole lot of knowledge about Minecraft to do well, because you have incredibly limited resources. If you screw up, you really can't fix it usually and will have to start all over.

This makes Skyblock one of the most respected forms of Minecrafting online today, because people know just how hard it is (most have tried and failed to get very far in it).

That being said, it just takes a little planning and thought to get a good, long game of Skyblock going. It's unlikely you'll complete the whole thing on the first go (very few could do this), but with our guide, you'll be on your way to a fully completed challenge list in just a match or two of this incredibly fun game.

LONG-FORM

Most minigames are short-lived things: meant to provide quick, fun entertainment for a half hour at most and a few minutes at the quickest.

The games in our Long-Form chapter are a different beast entirely. They are games designed to play and keep playing, where you go from having very little to months later being far advanced, and having a ton of stories to tell on the way.

Think of these kind of like Minecraft's MMORPG form. You and hundreds and even thousands of other players play in the same world and interact with it, building, warring, gaining experience, and all manner of other things for months on end.

When it comes to rewarding minigames (and those that take a bit of commitment), Long-Form minigames are at the top of the list.

CREATIVE

If you're more the type that likes to play Minecraft for the building and not the survival or combat, worry not: there are minigames out there for you, too. Creative minigames put the focus entirely on what you can do with blocks in this game, and they find ways to make it competitive so you can actually use your creative skills to win.

The Pixel Painters minigame, which involves drawing a picture of a certain subject using colored Wool.

These games are also absolutely top-notch training games to get better at building and become more creative, and only about one-third of people on them are actually any good, so they're not just for expert builders. Those of you who are just looking for some light fun, or who want to get better at building, should try them out as well.

Players wait in a lobby for their quirky game to start!

QUIRKY

Here's where we showcase all the minigames that just don't fit in any other category. Party games, goofy competitive games, and even a kart racing game can be found here, and there's very little in the way of difficult, complex rules to figure out.

These are the games you should check out when you just want to jump in and have some good, fast fun and take a break from all this serious Minecrafting in many of the other games. Each of them is very well done and there are usually tons of players online taking part in them, so you can always find someone else to get a bit goofy with.

Now that you know a bit about what kind of minigames there are, let's show you where to find 'em and get to playin'!

Where the Games Are:
Minigame Servers, and How to Get to Them

It's pretty hard to do some online Minecraft minigamin' if you don't know how to get on a server! Lucky for us all, it's super easy. **Here's how:**

Where (and How) to Add a Server

To add a server to your Minecraft server list so that you can access it whenever you like, follow these easy steps:

1. Open up Minecraft so you're looking at the main menu
2. Click "Multiplayer"
3. Click "Add Server"
4. Type in the address for the server you want to play on (more on finding addresses below)
5. Click "Done"
6. It will take you back to the page you were just on, and now your server will be at the bottom of that list
7. To join, click on the server in the list and then click "Join Server" at the bottom

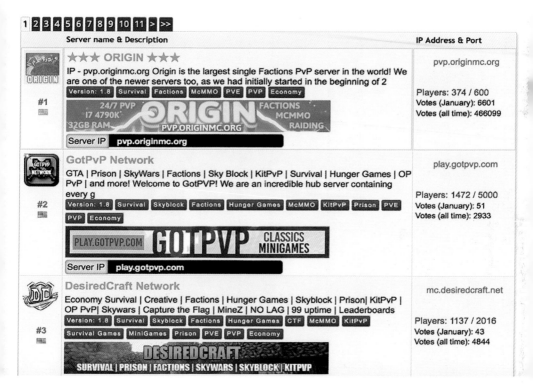

Server name & Description	IP Address & Port
★★★ ORIGIN ★★★ IP - pvp.originmc.org Origin is the largest single Factions PvP server in the world! We are one of the newer servers too, as we had initially started in the beginning of 2 Version: 1.8 | Survival | Factions | McMMO | PVE | PVP | Economy Server IP pvp.originmc.org	pvp.originmc.org Players: 374 / 600 Votes (January): 6601 Votes (all time): 466099
GotPvP Network GTA | Prison | SkyWars | Factions | Sky Block | KitPvP | Survival | Hunger Games | OP PvP | and more! Welcome to GotPVP! We are an incredible hub server containing every g Version: 1.8 | Survival | Skyblock | Factions | Hunger Games | McMMO | KitPvP | Prison | PVE | PVP | Economy Server IP play.gotpvp.com	play.gotpvp.com Players: 1472 / 5000 Votes (January): 51 Votes (all time): 2933
DesiredCraft Network Economy Survival | Creative | Factions | Hunger Games | Skyblock | Prison | KitPvP | OP PvP | Skywars | Capture the Flag | MineZ | NO LAG | 99 uptime | Leaderboards Version: 1.8 | Survival | Skyblock | Factions | Hunger Games | CTF | McMMO | KitPvP | Survival Games | MiniGames | Prison | PVE | PVP | Economy	mc.desiredcraft.net Players: 1137 / 2016 Votes (January): 43 Votes (all time): 4844

Finding Servers Online

You can't do much server-joining without knowing a server address or two. To do this is super easy:

Option A: Look through this book! We've included server addresses with every minigame in the book, all of which are top-notch servers.

Option B: Google the minigame you want to play, or simply "Minecraft server." A ton will come up, and server websites always have their server address plastered near the top of their homepage.

Option C: Use a Minecraft server list online. This is the best tool to use when finding a new server, as these sites show you everything from what games servers have on them to how many players are on right now to what the address for the server is in a very easy to read, searchable format.

GREAT MINECRAFT SERVER LISTS

- topg.org/Minecraft
- MinecraftServers.org
- FunMinecraftServers.com
- Minecraft-Server-List.com
- www.PlanetMinecraft.com/Resources/Servers

A Primer for Online Minecraft Play

Now, here's the thing about online Minecraft servers: they're busy, they're pretty complex, and they aren't very much like regular Minecraft at all.

You'll notice this from the minute you log into one. Instead of wilderness to the horizon or big, empty cities like many of the maps you can download for Minecraft, you're gonna see vibrant, bustling locations with giant signs, tons of decorations and more people than you've ever seen on Minecraft at once milling about, jumping around, and perhaps even exploding a bit (it does happen).

Even the interface for the game will be different, with new menus and buttons, and all this stuff in your inventory that doesn't quite do what it normally would.

All of this is normal and what makes a server work, but it's also more than a little overwhelming.

Fear not, Crafter, because this is your Primer to Servers, a short guide that'll get you at least a bit familiar with what you'll find on servers and will help you get around them and find fun things to do

NOTE: Every server is different, so this is just a basic walkthrough of common features, not a comprehensive guide. If you need help with something on a particular server, definitely don't hesitate to ask someone or go to their website to find what you need.

NAVIGATING SERVERS

The first thing you need to know about a server is how to get around it and where all these giant doorways go.

Servers are put together in a way that isn't totally apparent off the bat. Instead of everything on the server being in one giant world where you can visit the different sections like Disney Land, servers work more like train stations, or like the Ministry of Magic in Harry Potter.

You start out in a central location called the "hub," and this hub has different portals around the edges of it. Enter a portal, and you're teleported magically to a new section of the server, usually a minigame lobby or a survival world.

DEFINITIONS:

HUB: Hubs are the big, usually circular structures that you will be placed into when you first join most servers. From hubs you can get to smaller structures called lobbies either by choosing the lobby from your inventory or by walking through a portal. Hubs are the central location for servers and usually have the server's name done up big in fancy blocks with a lot of decorations. Hubs also usually have a lot of features dealing with character experience, donations, perks, and more that can be accessed, usually through talking to a Villager with a special label.

LOBBY: Lobbies are smaller structures you access from the hub that focus on one particular part of the server. Typically this is a minigame, but they can also be banks, shops, and other important locations. Lobbies usually have a lot of signs around them telling you about the lobby and offering access to things like shops, perk and experience menus, and, most importantly, minigame matches. Most minigames are joined by entering a lobby and then either using the inventory menus to join a game or finding the wall where matches are posted (they usually say the name of the minigame or map and then a number like "8/24" that represents the amount of players in the game and total available spots). You typically click on these signs to join a game.

Achievement get!
Taking Inventory

Crafting

, not have any pets, buy pets with xp at the xp shop
shotbow.net/forum/xp/shop

e to the Shotbow Xp System!

w XP lets you earn rewards in all Shotbow gamemodes
for playing, visit shotbow.net for more info.

Visit shotbow.net/forum/xp/shop to unlock rewards.

Your Inventory: You'll notice when you join a server that you have a ton of stuff already in your inventory and hot bar. These are usually not actual items (though sometimes they might be special items like Snowballs to throw at other players), but are instead actually menus. When you use them you'll activate the menu that the item is labeled with, such as "Join a Game." This will then give you a look at another inventory screen where there are more fake items that are also menu buttons. When you join a server for the first time, look through the various menus in the inventory and hot bar to see what your options are. Not all servers do this the same way, so you'll just need to check out your particular server and get familiar with how the menu system works.

Joining a Game: We've talked a bit about this already, but here's a very simple breakdown of the two ways you can typically go from entering a server's hub to playing a minigame

1. Join server > Open menu in inventory for the minigame lobby you want to join > Teleport to minigame lobby > Open the menu in the inventory for match lobbies for your minigame > Select an open lobby and join the match lobby > Teleport to match lobby > Wait for the match to start

The above two photos show the two different ways of actually joining a match. On top, players are selecting a match by clicking on the match's sign. On the bottom, you see a player picking a match from their inventory.

2. Join server > Walk through the portal for the minigame you want to play > Teleport to minigame lobby > Find the wall with matches listed > Select an open match and click the sign for it > Teleport to match lobby > Wait for match to start

You can also often do a combination of the two options above, choosing to walk to the portals from the hub and then use the inventory menus to join a match, or using the inventory to join a minigame lobby and then finding the wall with the matches.

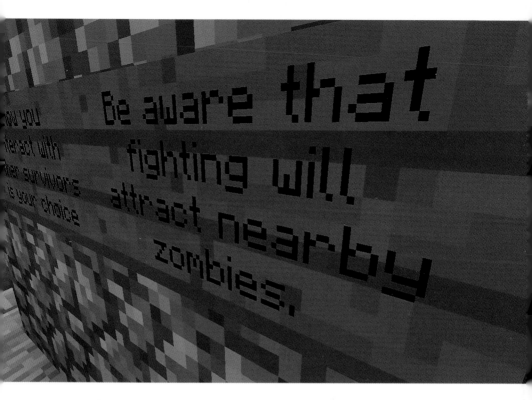

Be aware that fighting will attract nearby zombies.

ow you
teract with
her survivors
s your choice

MINIGAME RULES AND INSTRUCTIONS

One thing you might get confused about that is very important to playing on servers is how to actually play a minigame. You can easily join a minigame without ever having seen any instructions, and that's rarely fun, as a lot of them are very complex.

Not every server has an explanation for their minigames (smaller servers especially often just expect you to know what's up when you join), but most servers do, and their minigame rules and instructions almost always found in one of three places:

- In the minigame lobby on the walls as Signs. Many servers do this, and you can just run around the lobby reading them before you join a match.

- In your inventory in a Book. Another common feature—look in your inventory and see if there's a Book labeled with something about rules, instructions, or how to.

- On their website. Almost all big servers have websites, and most of those have an explanation of their minigames if not entire guides. If nothing else, you can also go on the forums on their site and ask around for help.

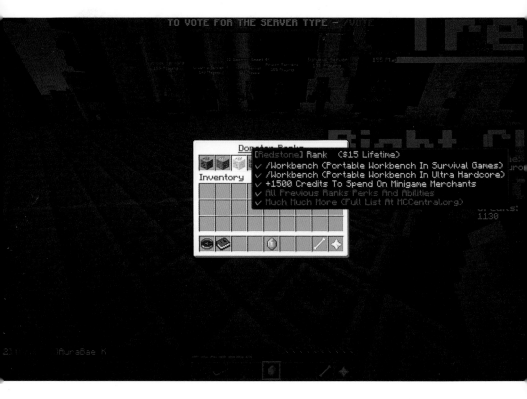

SERVER FEATURES FOR PLAYERS

Most servers, especially the top ones, have very extensive features for players such as experience points systems, currency systems, shops, ranks, and more. These are usually very complex and very specific to the server, but typically involve the player earning points by winning and/or participating in games, and also by donating money to the server or voting for the server on server listing sites online.

This is an important part of the server world because it's usually how you unlock cool features like being able to fly on a server or getting special kits to use in minigames, but each server is pretty different in the way they handle it. You can learn a lot about a server's features by looking around on the server itself or asking other players, but server websites are the easiest way to learn everything about your new favorite server and how to become a Super Mega Jedi Rank 1 Million on it.

Hypixel Network
Official Rules

All rules that are listed on this thread are now in effect as of October 2013 and apply to all ranks on the Hypixel Network. The following rules apply to the Hypixel Minecraft Servers, TeamSpeak, and Forums. All of the chat rules apply to any of our chat systems we have, an example of this would be private message or guild chat.

All users are to read and follow these rules to avoid the punishment of kick or ban. If for any reason a rule needs to be changed or modified, the Hypixel Administration has the right to do so.

Using an alternate account to avoid punishment such as a mute or ban is prohibited on the Hypixel network. If caught doing this, your ban/mute may be extended and the alternate account will be banned.

Respect All Staff Members
All decisions made by the Hypixel Staff Team are considered final. Please do not argue with a judgement made by one of our staff members. If you feel a member of staff is being abusive, please contact the Administration Team on the forums or message them privately.

SERVER ETIQUETTE (READ THIS, IT'S VERY IMPORTANT)

Over the years, millions of players have gotten on Minecraft servers to battle it out with each other, and through that time, a lot of trial and error has occurred that has led to the rules for big servers becoming pretty standard. While these aren't always the rules on every server, they will be on 95% of the servers you join, and you'll never get in trouble for following them on any server. You can and probably will not just get in trouble but totally banned from a server for breaking these rules, however, and that's never fun. It's best just to take these basic rules and follow them all the time to avoid any trouble:

1. No cursing. At all. Trust us on this one: it's pretty much a universal rule.

2. No harassing other people for any reason.

3. No spamming the chat.

4. The server staff is always in charge and always right. Don't yell at them, don't argue with them, don't mess with them.

5. Don't advertise anything on the server, even if it's Minecraft related or you think it's really cool.

6. Don't pretend to be on staff if you're not.

7. **NO CHEATING.** This cannot be stated enough. Do NOT use scripts, programs, or any other form of cheating. Not only is this not allowed and will get you banned, it's also rude and entirely ruins the point of minigames. Just don't do it, kids!

Survival-Based Games

There are other Minecraft minigames (this book is dang full of 'em!), but there really is no minigame out there that compares to the survival-based when it comes to competitiveness and lasting popularity. All of us play the same game that has the same rules as when playing in Survival Mode. Knowing those rules is essentially knowing Minecraft, and so it's no surprise that people would find it entertaining to engage each other in competitions based on surviving Minecraft while also killing those others out there that dare to presume they can survive better than you.

Survival-based minigames are some of the oldest, most difficult, and downright fiercest of the minigames available to this day, and, in fact, taking part in them is a time-honored tradition and a rite of passage in the world's most popular video game.

While there are as many ways to play a competitive survival game as there are coders to create them, there are a few modes of survival Minecraft that have cemented themselves as the banner-wavers for the genre in the online Minecraft community.

Survival Games

Basic idea: A quick version of *The Hunger Games* in Minecraft, complete with weapon Chests, starting columns for each player, and a last-man-standing-wins rule. One of the original Minecraft minigames, and the standard for PVP.

Number of players: Varies map-to-map and server to server

How long does it take: Depends entirely on the players and is different every time, but usually more than five minutes and less than thirty (however, this isn't always the case).

How hard is it: Again, depends on who you're playing with and whether you know the map, but it is usually very hard to win a

round because people have become very skilled at this minigame.

Where can it be found: Everywhere! Seriously—there's a variant of Survival Games on almost every server.

makenna01

```
urvivalGames | Tribute connermckay has fallen.
urvivalGames | 9 tributes remain.
urvivalGames | Tribute 2Ry2 has fallen.
urvivalGames | 8 tributes remain.
```

⚙ IMPORTANT FEATURES:

Perhaps the most popular game people have created within Minecraft, Survival Games involves special maps that have been created for combat. It's based on *The Hunger Games* books and films, and the idea is that a group of players start a battle to the death in a small arena near a bunch of Chests filled with various items. After a countdown, all players rush toward the items and try to grab as many as they can without getting killed, while also attacking other players.

Like books/movies, when you die, you're out, and the last player standing wins.

There are tons of these maps on servers and available to download online, but you can also try making your own! When playing online, make sure you read through the rules, as the type of items available and the things you can and can't do often varies depending on the server.

Basic Strategy for Winning: Winning at Survival Games is very hard, and a bit different than most of the other minigames you'll find in this book. This is because getting good at Survival Games takes two important strategies, one of which takes a good bit of time:

A. Use elite PVP methods and skills
B. Play with best Survival Games practices

PVP-ing the right way: Really when it comes down to what makes a good Survival Games player, knowing how to PVP is a lot of the battle. You need to know how to move, what items to use when, when to fight who, and when to run, as well as how to perform your attacks so that they do the most damage. Learning good PVP is something that takes a lot of practice at the general game of Minecraft, but here are some good tips that will especially help in Survival Games:

· Gear up and learn your gear. Don't fight without armor or a weapon and learn how to use every weapon there is so that you will be prepared to use whatever you find in the Chests. For instance, know how to use a Bow correctly, and realize that items like Fishing Rods and Flint and Steel can be among some of the best weapons out there (the Fishing Rod is awesome at causing players to fall off stuff!).

· Don't fight someone with better gear than you. If their armor is glowing with enchantments and yours is Leather, stay away.

· Move all the time when attacking. Circle your opponent, attack repeatedly when running at them, jump a lot, and generally don't give them anything still to target.

- Critical hitting is key. You can do much more damage in Minecraft if you hit someone while falling from a jump, so jump a lot while swinging. This is why you see people jumping a lot in combat, by the way (now you know!).

- Learn the maps to sneak attack people and use bottlenecks (places where people can only come at you one at a time). This is always key to any PVP match with standard maps, like Survival Games.

- Let other people kill each other off, and only engage one person at a time if possible. So, if you see people in a fight, just stay away until they damage each other if you can, and then swoop in and clean up whatever's left alive.

- Focus on gear and weapons before going into combat.

- Use the sneak key to your advantage. Players will be looking out for other players' nametags—hide yours by sneaking.

- Don't sprint when you're out of food. This is a quick way to lose health (because you need a full bar of food to regenerate health when you take damage). On that note, make sure you're gathering and eating food. Food is one of the most important and often overlooked parts of combat.

MINECRAFT TERMS:

Jitter clicking (aka, the blockhit). Jitter clicking is a term that refers to spamming the left mouse button then the right then the left again over and over while attacking with a Sword in Minecraft. Since the right mouse button blocks hits and the left attacks, this method can keep a lot of damage from hitting you while also doing a lot of damage to the opponent. It's super effective, especially when you get in a rhythm because you'll always be attacking when your opponent is knocked back from a hit and then blocking when they are attacking, but it can tire your hand out, so it takes some getting used to.

A Survival Games player hides from an enemy around a tree.

Here you see players engaged in the deathmatch at the end of the Survival Games, which teleports the last four remaining players to the map's original spawn area to settle the score.

- Avoid mobs, except those that you need to kill to get special items like Bones for Dogs from Skeletons.

- Set up your hotbar in a way that you are familiar with and which will allow you to access your weapons and health items (if you get so lucky as to have a Golden Apple or potions) FAST. You do not want to be wasting time with switching to the wrong item; you want to be able to go into combat mode without even thinking, spending all of your time hitting and avoiding/healing damage.

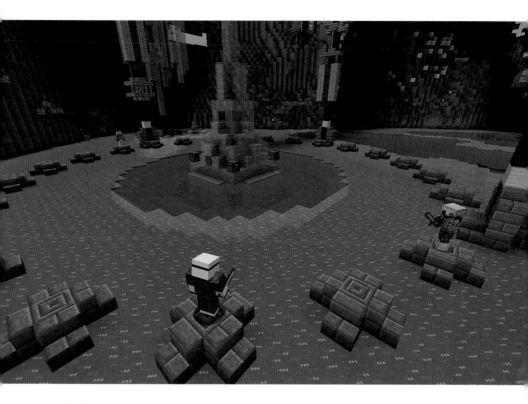

SURVIVAL GAMES TIPS FOR ELITE DESTRUCTION:

Here's the thing about Survival Games matches: you can play them just about any way you want, and you might get lucky and have a group of newbs that'll fall easily to your basic Minecraft attacks and strategies, but that's not very likely. Survival Games is super popular and has been around forever (at least, it feels like it), and people have gotten really good at it.

Over those years, many, many different strategies have been developed for kicking butt at Survival Games, and you'll see the players that win the most using them almost every time. To get to get to their level, you'll need to adopt at least a few of these elite strategies for yourself and make sure you use them every match.

- Avoid the "corn" 90% of the time. The corn is the cornucopia, better known to you as the big honkin' pile of Chests in the middle of the starting ring. While these Chests have items, you should almost always avoid them at the start of the game, because everyone else is going to charge at them as well. Then, it's just a game of luck and speed to see who gets what items, and who can equip weapons the fastest, before it turns into an all-out brawl. At best you'll get something good and get a kill or two but take a ton of damage, and at worst (and most of the time) you'll just get killed.

- Instead of going for the corn, run away from it as fast as you can and look for other Chests. These other Chests will have just as good of items as the corn, but they'll be away from the combat, allowing you to take more time to loot them and keeping you from damage.

- Equip smartly. If there are players right next to you, don't take the time to put on ALL of your gear unless you're really fast at it. Make sure you equip when you're safe and aren't going to be slaughtered while you're in your inventory screen.

- Don't advertise your gear. Having decent gear makes you a target: don't equip good armor until you have a weapon (equip a weapon immediately, though), and never ever tell people what you have. Even doing so to trick people is a bad idea, because it simply makes you a target.

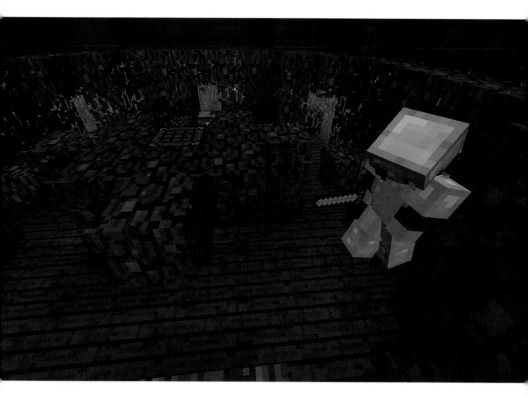

Waiting on the pylons before the Survival Games start (as seen here) is a tradition in this gamemode, and it's also a good time to plan your route.

LEARN MAPS AND CREATE ROUTES:

There is no better advice in all of Survival Games, and all good players do this. It takes playing a map a few times, but the very best thing you can do in this minigame is to know the map and know where you want to go each round. You want to create routes that go by where there are Chests (or where they are likely to be, if you're on a server where they spawn randomly), and then later when you're geared-up, you want to go where there are people. This is related to the next tip, which is...

Screenshot: Minecraft® ™ & © 2009–2016 Mojang/Notch

- Always be moving, unless you're sneaking and waiting to ambush someone. Standing around in an area is a good way to get killed, as players will notice you and will sneak attack you. Make this impossible by always being on the move.

- Hidden Chests and high-up Chests are most likely to have items still, Chests near spawn and out in the open are less likely to. Don't risk running across a field where you might be seen for a Chest that's out in the open near spawn, especially later in the game. Instead, look for a harder-to-reach or hidden Chest and stay safe.

- Team up if you want, but be careful. Many players will ask to be on teams before the fight. You can definitely do this, but also realize that your teammates may turn against you, and in the end, you'll have to fight them, too.

- If you find a Compass, use it. Compasses will point to the nearest other player during the day, and to supply drops at night.

- Enchant your weapons and armor if you can find the table. You should be racking up a lot of experience points during Survival Games, and it is absolutely worth it to enchant if you know where a table is.

- Try to train a Dog or two. This is one of the best elite tricks in Survival Games: if you can get some Bones, definitely look for a Wolf and tame it. It'll become your personal attack Dog, and your secret weapon against your enemies. Remember though: you need to engage another player in combat yourself before your Dog will attack them.

- Be ready to deathmatch at the end of the game. When there are four or fewer players left, many servers institute a deathmatch round to end the game. This involves teleporting all the remaining players to the original spawn, where they must duke it out in a free-for-all, the winner of which wins the match. Be ready for this with good gear and practiced PVP skills, and you'll greatly increase your chances of coming out on top. Oh, and remember: if they made it that far, they're probably pretty good themselves.

Blitz

Basic idea: A faster and wilder Survival Games variant.

Number of players: 16-32

How long does it take: Less than five minutes

How hard is it: If you find regular Survival Games hard, this will be even harder because it's more chaotic and cramped.

Where can it be found: mc.hypixel.net

⚙ IMPORTANT FEATURES:

Survival Games is one of the most popular minigames, and it has been for a long time, but Blitz is our favorite version of Survival Games. It takes the basic Survival Games concept of an arena with Chests with items scattered around it and kit selection and makes the competition much fiercer and quicker by having smaller arenas, crazier kits, and a special Blitz Star that spawns every so often and gives the finder extra powers.

Games of Blitz start out like other Survival Games matches, with players spread out evenly in a circle around a group of Chests. When the countdown finishes, players are able to move and can either risk running to the Chests to try to get items before other players, or they can just run off into the map. PVP is immediately enabled in Blitz, but the items from your kit won't appear in your inventory until 60 seconds into the match. The arenas are small but have many hiding spots, and they also contain quite a few hidden Chests.

Combine all of this together, and you get a very complex game that moves much quicker than regular Survival Games (which can sometimes go on for a very long time). Typically many players are killed in the first 60 seconds of each match (before they even get their kits), but the last few players in a game of Blitz can often still take a decent amount of time to pick each other off.

While Survival Games is still going strong as one of the top minigames for Minecraft, we think Blitz gives it a little kick-in-the-pants both in terms of pacing and complexity (with the addition of the Blitz Star and better kits) that makes us favor it over the original. Of course, that's not too surprising considering that this minigame is one of the always-great Hypixel server creations.

Basic Strategy for Winning: Strategy in Blitz is fairly complex and requires quick changes and thinking. You'll have to decide whether to risk going for Chests or simply to hide and wait for your kit, and you'll be playing against all sorts of other kits, including those that are far above your level. Being higher level does not necessarily guarantee a kill in Blitz, though; it's still pretty easy to kill someone who has a good kit if you catch them at the right time with the right items (especially before they get their kit).

There are a ton of kits in Blitz (far too many to list here), each of which has very specific traits and powers, and each of which can be upgraded from level I to level X. Some of the kits are free, while others require winning and purchasing to access. The level of the kit determines the amount and quality of items you get from it and your appearance.

You also have a player tracker in the form of a compass, which will show you the direction of the closest player, which can help both offensively and defensively.

The Blitz Star, while not a game breaker, certainly is a game changer, as it spawns randomly on the map every five minutes and allows the finder to select from a variety of special one-time boosts. There are 18 of these, and they can do everything from teleporting to the closest player and dealing 10 damage, making all arrows one-shot-kill for a 30 second period, steal hit points from players in a radius around the player, or give extra regeneration, and much more. All Blitz Stars also give Regeneration II for 30 seconds, which is useful all on its own.

💡 TIPS FOR PROS:

· Kits drop at one minute into the match.

· The Blitz Star spawns somewhere on the map every five minutes.

· This game is much faster than regular Survival Games, so it's much more important to keep on the move than in regular Survival Games.

· It will take a few times at least to get familiar with the various kits and Blitz Star bonuses. To get truly good at this game, you'll have to practice quite a bit.

The Walls

Basic idea: Four teams of players start out separated from each other and must mine resources and build tools. After a set amount of time, the walls between each team drop and the teams enter a PVP contest where the last team with a living player wins.

Number of players: Usually around 20-34

How long does it take: 10-30+ minutes

How hard is it: If you get a good team and the enemy doesn't know the game, this can be won easily, but otherwise it's of medium to hard difficulty to win.

Where can it be found: Many! This is another of the most popular Minecraft styles, and many servers (including many of the most popular servers) have this minigame on their rotation. That being said, Hypixel created this game, and mc.hypixel.net is the home of The Walls.

⚙ IMPORTANT FEATURES:

One of the very most popular and commonly found minigames, The Walls is another by the legendary Hypixel. This time around we've got a survival-based team PVP match with a twist:

You and 3 other players or teams are dropped into one quadrant of a regular Minecraft world that has limits (meaning it's only so big). There are giant sand walls dividing your quadrant of the map from the other players, and a huge timer floating above everything. You have the time until the timer reaches 0:00 to prepare yourself and your area for battle, and once the timer does hit zero, the walls fall down!

At that point, it's an all-out brawl to see who can live the longest. Whoever does, wins it all.

Basic Strategy for Winning: The Walls is all about building up a hotbar and inventory of good gear as fast as possible and helping your teammates to get gear of their own. The only real strategy is to gear up as fast as possible, which means taking the basic tenants of Minecraft (chop wood, make tools and weapons, dig stone, make better tools, dig ore, make better tools, weapons and armor) and doing them as fast as you can. It helps to be communicating with your teammates and splitting up the jobs (someone keeps looking for food and chopping wood while someone else mines ore etc.), but you can also take on the task on your own if you need to. Essentially, you just want to be the most well-geared person in terms of Swords and Armor when the walls drop.

Walls maps can get pretty creative looking, but the essentials of the game stay the same.

♥ TIPS FOR PROS:

- You're not allowed to leave the designated map area, nor are you allowed to build over the height of the walls or knock down any of the wall on your own. Doing so will get you disqualified, so stick to the rules, kiddo.

- Go for an Iron Pickaxe and then an Iron Sword first. The pickaxe will massively speed up your resource collection speed, which will end up making you more powerful in the end (as long as you hit veins of ore), and the Sword will be your protection. After that, go for armor as fast as you can and keep replacing your sword and pickaxe as needed.

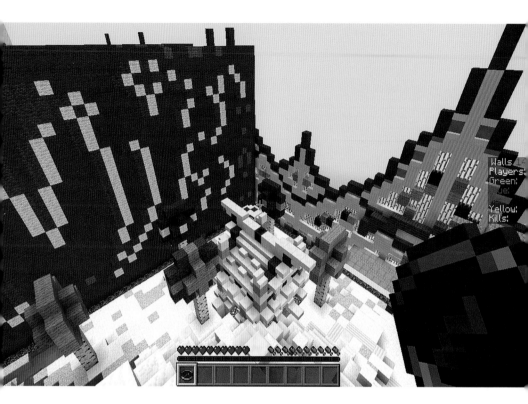

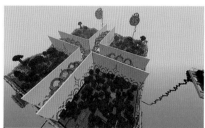

This is the traditional walls set-up, but with an added twist of having temples with extra items and resources between the walls (instead of just having a one-block wall separating the quadrants).

- Talk to your team and be as organized as possible.

- Keep a lookout for other players, and always keep them in mind. Sometimes invading enemy territory when you aren't feeling quite ready is a good idea if done early after the walls have fallen, because the other team might not expect you yet.

- For the most part, play with the idea of having an awesome final showdown in mind (so gear up constantly) rather than spending time hunting players. Gear wins this game.

Ultra Hardcore

Basic idea: A set of players is dropped into a randomly generated Minecraft survival world and has to craft their own gear and battle to the death, last man standing style. It's the ultimate Minecraft skills minigame.

Number of players: 80-100

How long does it take: A while, with the right set of players. Sometimes a player can come around and slaughter the others quickly, or if you're playin' with newbs some of them might fall to their deaths or get killed by a mob pretty quick for an under 15 minute game. Sometimes, though, you'll get a match full of Minecraft gurus and it'll go for hours. It just depends, though it does trend faster than slower.

How hard is it: Hard. If you're playing against good players, as hard as it gets. But also, it's regular Minecraft, so you can use the skills you've built in the regular game to do this. The difficulty varies based on the skills of your opponents and also the random factors that might hit you or other players.

Where can it be found: mc.hypixel.net, play.reevemc.com, ex.gg, mc.uhc.zone

A Guide To Winning Ultra Hardcore:

If horse racing is the sport of kings, Ultra Hardcore or UHC is the minigame of Minecraft monarchs. By that we mean it's the game for the very best of the best when it comes to Minecraft, and only those players who truly know what they're doing in survival mode can ever hope to last for more than 20 minutes or so, much less win a game of UHC. Check out the YouTube channels of any member of the Mindcrack Network, which regularly engages in riveting UHC brawls, to see the kind of skills it takes to get good at this minigame.

What makes UHC so gosh darned hard? Well, that'd be in the name: it's not just Hardcore Mode, which means one death and you're out, it's Ultra Hardcore mode, which makes it hard to impossible to heal. Otherwise it's a fight to the death in Survival Mode, typically on a small (and sometimes shrinking!) map, but the fact that you have to be very careful not to even lose one heart carelessly is what makes UHC so hard and so thrilling.

While learning to be the best of the best at UHC requires mastery of just about all things Survival, meaning you'll want to simply learn all you can about the game, this is a mini-guide to the mode that will give you a leg up on your opponents and make you much more likely to survive. Remember though: these are just tips! UHC is all about general Minecraft knowledge and adaptability, so make sure to learn about the basics of the game as well, and never be afraid to try a bold new strategy if it makes sense in the situation.

NOTE:

Hiding your achievements is an excellent UHC strategy, because knowing what another player is doing is extremely helpful to defeating them in this mode. You can do this by having just one player on a team craft all of your Crafting Tables, handing them out to the other players. You get the "Benchmarking" achievement only when you pick up a Crafting Table from the output slot of either your inventory crafting menu or from a Crafting Table output. Since you have to get achievements in a specific order in order to get the next one, skipping the Benchmarking achievement will mean that your achievements stop showing, even if you complete the necessary action. This will help spread confusion and disinformation, giving you a distinct advantage. Does not work in single player UHC, however, unless you steal someone else's Crafting Table.

1. Don't waste time, especially at the beginning. You simply can't mess around when playing UHC, especially right at the beginning. While later stages of the match are harder to do with perfect efficiency, like Diamond/Gold hunting or Arrow creating, everything you need to do at the beginning can be done right or wrong. That is to say, you can be quick about it, or you can do it badly. When you start a match of UHC, you need to acquire food, Wood, Crafting Tables, and basic gear as quickly as you can, or else another team or competitor will be ahead of you and thus much more likely to win.

2. Know the specific rules of the server and the match. Not all UHC matches are the same. Some spawn you with a gear kit, some have shrinking borders, some allow healing with potions while others only allow it with Golden Apples or not at all. Know the rules of the specific server you're on and the match you're in, or else you may spend a lot of time trying to do something that just won't work.

3. Be overly careful. Do not take damage from anything except a player or a mob, and avoid that at all costs. Falling damage or damage from Lava, drowning or hitting a teammate is really something that should not happen in a UHC match, and if it does, it means you are less likely to win. Paranoia based security is the name of the game: if it seems even a little dangerous, get away from it ASAP. Do not make risky jumps if possible, stay out of dark places when possible (even dark forests) and run away from all hostile mobs (especially Skeletons), don't even get near Lava in most situations. It's just not worth it unless you have awesome armor, which you won't for a while.

4. Get the right resources, ignore the others. Not everything is useful in UHC. Here's a list of things you want, everything else can be ignored or dropped for the most part:

Raw resources:
- Wood, Coal, Iron, Gold, Diamond, Emerald (Emerald only in case you see a Village), Lapis Lazuli (for enchanting in v1.8 or above)
- Food, especially Apples but do not eat Apples (they are for making Golden Apples)
- Feathers and Flint (for Arrows)
- Sugar Cane and Leather (to make Books for enchanting)
- Obsidian (for Enchanting Table, best made instead of hunted)
- String (for Bows)

Specialty items for specific strategies:
- Bones (to tame Wolves who will fight for you)
- Brewing items (Sand/Glass, Blaze Rods, and Nether Wart, etc., to make Potions. Very, very dangerous but can work if done carefully.)

5. Go underground quickly. Once you've gathered whatever food you can on the surface and have plenty of Wood, Crafting Tables, and basic tools, you need to get underground and start hunting ores and Spiders ASAP. The best option is to find caves and follow them, or safely go down a ravine, but if you can't find any of these quickly, go ahead and just start digging down in a staircase. You need ore, because as our next step says...

6. Gear is essential. Gear is what will make you win or lose UHC. Outside of ambushes and accidents, the people with the best gear almost always win the match, so it is your number one priority. Gear is important in the following order, with the most important at the the top, and you would do well to focus on acquiring each in this order

- Stone Sword and tools
- Armor (the best kind you can make)
- Food
- Better Sword, and Bow and Arrows (equally important)
- Golden Apples
- Potions

7. Consider the Nether. This is very risky, but there are also massive benefits if you survive. The Nether will put you away from most other players, who will be scared to venture there, and it will give you the opportunity to collect Blaze Rods and Nether Wart to make potions. However, do not go to the Nether if you are not very, very good at surviving in it, and never go without at least Iron Armor, a Bow, and an Iron Sword, if not better gear.

8. Be sneaky and vigilant at all times. Many players in UHC get killed simply because they were focusing too much on resource hunting and gear crafting and they didn't notice that someone was sneaking up on them. Make sure you're scanning your surroundings for other players at all times, and try to stay out of sight or underground whenever possible. Also, use the darkness trick to see other players' nametags: dig a hole or place blocks on all sides of you so that you are in total darkness, then look in every direction. If there is any player near you, you'll see a nametag. Beware though; other players use this trick, so if you think someone might be looking for you, go into sneak mode with the crouch key. This hides your nametag, allowing you to remain safely hidden.

9. Pay attention to coordinates. It's a good idea to keep your coordinates up and watch them at all times. This is because you want to know where you've been in order not to go over the same area repeatedly, and so you know where you are in relation to the center of the map. The center is where players will most often have to pass through, making it the most dangerous area as well as the best hunting grounds. This strategy is especially important for matches with shrinking maps.

10. Bring the fight to the enemy. When you're all geared up, don't just wait around for other players to ambush. Do this some, but do it on the move. A player that's moving is much harder to target and is much more likely to get the drop on other players and defeat them. If you're geared up, be bold and take the fight to your enemies, but of course do this stealthily and carefully.

There is little in Minecraft as rewarding as outsmarting, out-surviving, and simply outcrafting everyone else in a UHC match. It's thrilling, nail-biting fun that we can't recommend enough, and with this little guide, you are much more likely to come out on top.

NOTE: This is not as common a game on servers as some of the other minigames, primarily because it's challenging, but also because it takes a bit of time and quite a few people to play. A match can last anywhere from 30 minutes to three or four hours, and it's best played with at least 8 people or 4 teams. That being said, it's the pinnacle of Minecraft competition, and it should be played by all Crafters.

💡 TIPS FOR PROS:

· Gear up to the best of your abilities.

· Watch your back all the time. Rotate a full circle as often as you can looking for other players or nametags.

· Play the game like you normally would, but really fast and focusing on gear, not building.

· Look for caves. You need ore above almost everything else (except Bows and Apples). Caves and ravines are a necessity.

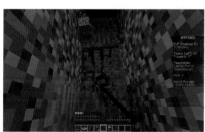

- If you find Apples, DO NOT EAT THEM. Also, look for Gold and don't use it unless you're building a Golden Apple. These are perhaps the most useful items later in the game of UHC, because they will give you a health boost and start to heal you.

- Use Golden Apples before any fight if possible, or as early in it as you think you'll need it. You don't want to have one of these bad boys and get killed without eating it. This is a hard thing to time, but you can get better at it if you think about using it as soon as you know you'll be in combat soon. You can also use Golden Apples to heal when not in combat if your health is dangerously low.

Parkour and Minecraft Servers

All along the walls and across the landscape of the many different servers out there in the universe of Minecraft, and often along their very own maps, you'll find these funny little blocks floating in clusters that string around the area. On top of these blocks that often float above the milling crowds of avatars on a server, you'll often see players, hopping from block to block determinedly. Hopping, and almost always falling down to join the rest of the crowd, but then heading straight back to hop back up on these precarious obstacle courses that are so commonly found on multiplayer servers.

What are they doing, and what are these little clusters of blocks?

Everyone's Favorite "Minigame": Parkour

It's called Parkour, and it's one of Minecraft's most beloved and common "minigames." We put minigames in quotes here because, unlike most minigames in this book, Parkour doesn't require a bunch of special game rooms or coding to play or set up, nor does it have an automatic "scoring" mechanism, leaderboards, or any recognition for the "winners" other than their own personal satisfaction in their Minecraft skills.

Parkour is jumping across paths that are built in the sky across a Minecraft map and that usually involve jumping from just one single block to land on another. They also often have special trick areas where you have to land on the side of a block with a single piece of Ladder on it, sometimes even jumping from this precarious position to the next part of the course.

Parkour courses can be anything from an actual minigame set up with its own fancy map and server, maybe even with some Redstone scoring or other mechanisms set up, or it can just be a few blocks set up in a course on part of a map. Because it's so easy to set up, you'll find Parkour everywhere on servers, with many servers even building little Parkour courses across their spawn hubs or in minigame waiting rooms.

How to Get Better at Parkour

Being good at Parkour is a bit of a badge of honor among Minecraft players online, and just about everyone gives it a shot. All you're trying to do in Parkour is to jump from block to block on a pre-made course while not falling. If you fall, the courses are set up so that you have to start all the way over at the beginning, and if you make it to the end, you win! However, being that accurate with jumps is much harder than it looks, though with a little practice you'll find yourself getting better and better.

Getting to be good at Parkour, like with most things Minecraft and otherwise, is mostly about practicing again and again. Here's a quick guide to how you can speed up that learning process, along with a few pro tricks to help you out

1. Change your sprint to a different key, instead of having it be double tapping forward. Double tapping forward to sprint is clunky and hard to time, especially when you only have a single block to jump from in most Parkour jumps. Change it to something you can easily hold while running forward, like the left shift key.

Not all Parkour courses have the same aesthetic. While the single block/column method of making Parkour maps has come to dominate the aesthetic landscape for this minigame, any map where the point is to create a difficult course that takes skill in jumping to navigate is a Parkour map.

2. Learn to jump accurately both from a regular position and from a running start. A jump from a regular run (not sprinting) can take you a maximum of 2 blocks forward. A jump from a sprint will take you 4 blocks forward maximum. When calculating whether you need to sprint or not, keep in mind that you need to add not just the distance straight out from you to your target, but the distance up too, if it's above you. Learning to sprint and jump from a 1 block wide platform is hard enough, and learning to land on another 1 block wide platform is even harder. You can try it on regular online Parkour courses that you find around servers, or you can use our next step for a more private and less stressful way to train.

A very extensive single-player Parkour map based on the *Assassin's Creed* video game series seen from above.

3. Learn to jump from the very edge of a block. This is especially important when trying to make a 4 block jump, and you can learn to do it by looking straight down when jumping. Later, when you get the timing down, you can look forward while doing it so that you can aim your jump better.

🔥 **HOT TIP:** Jumping diagonally is different than going straight forward in Minecraft. The maximum distance for diagonal jumps is just 3 blocks when sprinting. That includes distances up, though you can make a diagonal jump of more than 4 blocks distance when falling.

4. Find some Parkour maps online and download them to practice at home. That, or building a small course for yourself is absolutely the best way to learn how to make these kind of jumps (though you probably won't build something quite as difficult or complex as many of the online Parkour courses for your first go at it). The other players and the pressure of playing the difficult online courses makes it pretty hard to practice Parkour online, while doing so in the privacy of your own game can really help you learn to gauge the distances and get them down pat. Focus on regular jumps first, then try out some of the difficult ones like Ladder jumps, or jumps when a block is right above the block you're jumping from (meaning you absolutely have to sprint off it). If there's a particular jump you're having trouble with, build just that one right on the ground and try it over and over, so that it's easier to keep restarting just that jump (you don't have to get all the way to that part of the course to try it).

5. Practice jumping in other parts of Minecraft! This is an often-overlooked idea, but it's really smart. When you're playing your other favorite types of Minecraft, even vanilla survival, practice making jumps and really think about what you're doing when you do or don't make them. Minigames like TNT Run where there's a lot of jumping can be super helpful in this.

Some Parkour maps like this one are set up for speed runs, a term that means the point isn't just to get through it, but to get through it fast. They often have timers and leaderboards so that players can see how they stack up against other Parkour enthusiasts.

6. Look for shortcuts in the map where you can jump from a block over another section of the map. This isn't considered cheating; it's considered smart Parkour!

7. Remember that you can't fall off a block while sneaking. Hold the sneak key down while you're between jumps so that you can plan your next jump, get more distance to sprint (by sneaking backwards to the edge of your current block farthest from your target) and relax for a second without the worry of falling off.

8. When you've got all of the regular jumps down pat, try out some of the really hard ones that are out there, like the dreaded Stairs jump, Water jumps, or even Soul Sand jumps. These are incredibly tricky, and you won't see them in most Parkour courses, but they are out there on some of the most pro Parkour spots. If you can learn to do these well, you'll be a Parkour master.

🔥 HOT TIP: Hit the crouch/sneak key when you are trying to land on a Ladder or Vines in Parkour. This will automatically make you "stick" to the Ladder or Vines and not fall, which makes these jumps oh so much easier (and is actually required with Vine jumps). Crouching when landing is also important for jumping around corners, as you can hit the "box" that the block has for you to stand on (each item in the game has an invisible box like this which is what you actually stand on).

Top Parkour Destinations and Maps

Intrigued by this most favorite of Minecraft minigames? Or maybe you're a hardcore Parkour-ist and you're lookin' for a shiny new course to challenge your skills on? Here are some awesome ideas for places to go to find your new favorite Parkour courses online, and a couple profiles of awesome Parkour maps to download.

Great Parkour Servers

- mc.hypixel.net
- play.cubecraft.net
- play.dubcraft.org
- play.planetmine.org
- mc.arkhamnetwork.org
- pvp.desteria.com
- mc.parkourcraft.com
- us.mineplex.com
- play.lemoncloud.org
- play.itsjerryandharry.com
- play.skybattle.net

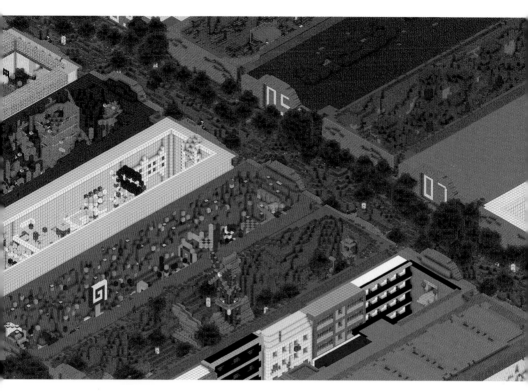

Parkour Map Christmas Calendar

This particular map features a whole heap of various parkour areas, each with its own theme and difficulty level. It was created by the MinecraftPG5 group as a Christmas release, and it is an absolutely top-notch example of the parkour style.

By MinecraftPG5: Certainly one of the most popular types of mini-games, the concept of parkour is simple and easy to pick up, but hard to master. Essentially, it's just jumping and otherwise maneuvering from a starting point to a goal without falling. If you fall, you start over!

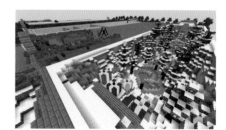

Minecraft Game Show

Fans of the TV show Wipeout will recognize this instantly, and guess what? It all works! If you aren't a person who watches wacky TV shows where people have to bounce across obstacle courses, that's basically what happens in Wipeout, and Nboss233 has made this one work basically the way the TV show does. It's kind of like parkour maps, in that you

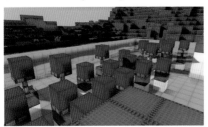

mostly are jumping from thing to thing and trying not to fall, and there are a ton of moving parts and crazy obstacles to get through. What's maybe most impressive about it, besides how well they nailed the look of the show, is that there is a giant digital timer on one side that will actually keep track of how fast everyone does it!

Herobrine Boss

"Boss battles" are a type of minigame that basically involve having a big crafted character as the central figure for a series of challenges, usually waves of mobs. SpeedyCrafting and his crew are known for creating such battles, and this is one that they've said is much harder than some of their earlier creations. From the PlanetMinecraft entry, here's what you'll be facing if you dare to challenge the dark and dangerous Herobrine (Minecraft's biggest legend):

Wave 1: [Easy] Parkour & hit all of the redstone lamps. The door to Wave 2 will open when you've hit the 4 redstone lamps.

Wave 2: [Hard!] Parkour & flip the right levers. The levers are on Herobrine's body. the door to Wave 3 will open when you've hit the 3 right levers.

Wave 3: [Hard Too!] Wave 3 is a 1 vs 1, face to face battle with Herobrine (like in the picture). You have to climb into his head and smash 23 mobs into his neck (the creeper-face hole). Press the pressure plate on the wooden "chest" to spawn the mobs. When you've smashed the 23 mobs in it, Herobrine will explode and his eyes will stop glowing.

Player vs. Player
Games

Minecraft was never really meant to be an epic combat game, with its simple graphics and user interface, but fighting always has been a part of our blocky game. That, plus the love gamers have for smacking things with swords and shooting each other up with whatever weapons are around, should make it no surprise then that when online Minecraft play went big-time with giant servers full of people and heavily modified versions of the game, Player-vs-Player became one of the game's most popular modes.

These days, PVP minigames are perhaps the most popular style that there is. Technically, many of the other games in this book are PVP too (Survival Games, UHC, Factions, etc.), but there are so many specifically PVP games that are more about the killing and less about another goal or feature that our biggest chapter in the book is focused all on PVP.

Here you'll find a collection of the baddest, roughest, most chaotic PVP minigames in all of Minecraft. These are the games you want to play if laying waste to your enemies and coming out on top of a pile of virtual bodies sounds like good clean fun to you. Each one is handpicked by our staff of experts out of the endless pile of PVP games online to bring to you the very best of the best, so give these guys a try, and see how your mettle stands up to the best PVP players in the world.

Annihilation

Basic idea: Four teams of players each have a base where they spawn and which contains a "nexus" that the team must defend while trying to destroy the nexus of the other teams.

Number of players: Up to 120!

How long does it take: This is a much longer PVP than most, and can last over 30 minutes.

How hard is it: Actually not too difficult to play. Everyone has a chance to kill other players and help fight or defend the nexus, and you can use your regular Minecraft skills to help your team a lot by gathering resources.

Where can it be found: us.shotbow.net

Map: Aftern▪
Blue Nexus:
Green Nexus:
Red Nexus:
Yellow Nexus:
Current Phas

Phase 1 – 2:52

nter13CA5ND killed 6Lord(5CP)
nter13CA5ND killed tithefirst(5PY)

⚙ IMPORTANT FEATURES:

Annihilation is a cool version of PVP that pits very large amounts of players against each other in a hybrid of survival Minecraft and an FPS "base defense" style PVP match. Essentially, each team has a giant, very well fortified base where they spawn and can do work like creating armor and weapons, and each base has a special room in it where a series of blocks make up the "nexus" for the base.

The overall goal is to protect your team's nexus while attacking the players and nexus of the three other teams. Whichever team's nexus survives the longest wins, and the game progresses in 10-minute phases, each of which has different features (such as the nexus becoming attackable in Phase 2).

THE PHASES OF ANNIHILATION

PHASE 1: Nexus blocks are invincible, only players can take damage.

PHASE 2: Players can attack the nexus blocks.

PHASE 3: Witches spawn on the map, and Diamond Ore (!) is spawned into the middle of the map to fight over.

PHASE 4: Can buy Blaze Powder at the potion shop on the map, and a Wither spawns.

PHASE 5: Damage done to the nexus is doubled for the rest of the game.

CracksHD(ACR) killed Infinite_Love_14(PYR)
e231(SCO) killed MeesGam3r2005(MIND)
JcAndrew(DEF) killed 3mike231(SCO)
McFlyHD(SCP) killed Chino_Love(ASN) defending Blue's Nexu

ewhale_Sea(SCO) killed Witherboss7(ARC)

Map: Afte
Green Nexu
Yellow Nexu
Blue Nexus
Red Nexust
Current Ph

Basic Strategy for Winning: Despite being a pretty straightforward PVP game, there's actually a lot going on in Annihilation, and a lot that goes into winning.

For one, each player has a class, and there are 37 different classes that you can choose from. Most of them need to be unlocked using server experience/currency, but you should have 1-4 available to you from the beginning. Knowing your class and targeting certain classes to unlock is very helpful in Annihilation.

When it comes to actual gameplay, it's important to decide what role on the team you want to play. Typically, players either defend and build resources for the team, go for the middle (especially when the Diamonds drop), or they attack the other team and its nexus. Picking a role and sticking to it will be very helpful to your team, though you should also jump in to help where needed (say if your nexus is under heavy attack and needs some extra defenders).

Gathering resources is very important in Annihilation, and is done in a way that's somewhat similar to Prison. You still need regular correct tools to mine and gather, but instead of going out into the wilderness to find your resources in a regular survival manner, you'll need to find the mines situated around your base to get each different resource. There will be a pile of logs, for instance, to get Wood, and a mine each for Iron, Gold, Redstone and Emerald. The resources will respawn quickly after you mine them, and you can stay and mine as long as you need (though be courteous to others mining and don't take every block of ore for yourself).

Learning to navigate Annihilation maps is of particular importance. Knowing where the routes are between bases, as well as where the exact middle of the map is, becomes of utmost importance in a minigame that is all about being in the right place at the right time to do damage to the right team (typically the one with the least amount of health in its nexus).

Shops are important in Annihilation: you'll find shops in your base, and you can use smelted Gold Ingots at the shop to buy all manner of useful and important items, many of which you can't get elsewhere.

Being the team to take control of the resources released with the different phases is important in Annihilation, because they will give the controlling team a major advantage. Diamonds only spawn in the middle with Phase 3, for instance, and the Wither boss that drops in Phase 4 will give the team that gets the killing blow a special "Boss Buff Star" each, which can be traded in at a special shop for "legendary" items.

Don't skimp on the forging, crafting, and resource-gathering in Annihilation! These are key to winning, as you need to really gear up and help your team do so to be competitive (other teams will be doing this, you can be sure).

💡 TIPS FOR PROS:

· Learning the maps is very important in Annihilation, both so you know the best paths to bases and the center of the map and so that you know how to find the nexus. Spend some time finding your own nexus when on a new map so that you know where to go in the other bases (it will be in the same place in the other teams' bases), or go online to the Shotbow page to look at maps of the levels.

· Nexus blocks have 75 hit points and they break much faster using Pickaxes. To really speed things up, use the fastest Pickaxe: the Golden Pickaxe.

Learning to use a Bow well can be deeply helpful in Annihilation. Get shootin' on some mobs in creative mode to get better!

- You don't have to run all the way to the enemy base the regular way—build a bridge or a tunnel to sneak attack!

- It's more important to protect your own nexus than do just about anything else. Run back to it when you see it's being attacked, or use the /kill command to die but be teleported right back to your base to help out.

- Adding your own walls and fortifications is important in Annihilation. You want to make it as hard as possible for the other team to reach your nexus, but as easy as you can for your own team to get to it to defend. Build around spawn, and make layers of walls using different materials so that the other team has to keep switching tools to get through your walls quickly.

silverlake12

ning CTF1!
do not have added any friends on Lichcraft, /friend to
e more

Capture the Flag

We just can't say it enough for PVP games (or most others): learn your map. You should be able to tell exactly what room you're in during CTF just by what it looks like, and know how to get to where you need to go.

Basic idea: Your standard team-based first-person capture-the-flag game, including PVP combat and needing to sneak into the other base to get the enemy flag before returning it to your own base.

Number of players: Any and varies by server, but 10 or more is really a good idea.

How long does it take: Highly variable, but usually at least 15 minutes

How hard is it: One of the simplest games in terms of features and strategy, but one of the most exciting and epic to play

Where can it be found: mc.desiredcraft.net, us.mineplex.com, mc-central.net, mc.arkhamnetwork.org, mcbrawl.com, mc.parkercraft.it, and a whole lot more!

⚙ IMPORTANT FEATURES:

Capture the Flag is pretty much ubiquitous in competitive video gaming, especially in first-person games, because it's just such a balanced and compelling way to game. Having an objective that can either be roving (when the flag is stolen) or stationary (when securely in the base or dropped) forces players to constantly be battling over different parts of a giant map, using different tactics all the time. This makes for a very fluid game with lots of unexpected and unpredictable moments, and in Minecraft's version, this is no different.

The premise is essentially the exact same as in most other CTF games: each team has a base with a flag room and a flag, and you want to get to the other team's flag and run over it to pick it up. You then need to return it to your own flag room to "capture" it. As soon as you pick up the flag, though, the enemies will be notified (which includes your player name), and they'll be coming for you en masse. While going for the other team's flag, you'll need to be defending your own, trying to keep players from picking it up, and killing any that do.

Depending on the server, there may be additional features to your CTF matches, including special kits, powerups and features like a dropped flag being returnable or returning on its own to your base after a certain amount of time.

Basic Strategy for Winning: Really there are just three parts to CTF strategy, and they're the same for all games (not just Minecraft): Learn the maps, pick a role, and know any special features or powers that are available.

Learning the map is by far the most important part of the game. Knowing routes to the other base, where the flag is, and how to get back to your own base without getting caught are essential. This really just comes with experience, so play a map a few times and take mental notes (or even real ones) of where things are and what paths work and what don't.

Picking a role and sticking to it is incredibly important to CTF. For instance, this is the middle of a CTF map. Hanging out here for most of the game would be to take a "mid" role, which is a very important and often-overlooked component to a CTF win.

Red 1 ‖ 1 Blue

Sh1lizzite's powerful stone sword finished slurpdog123
monkeyboy294: xD rewkting blue left and right
Top 5 Kills =====
nkeyboy294: 26
wondorks: 20
c_cake_27: 16
o_Playz_MC: 10
ndo2347: 8

This is a special feature you'll find in some CTF maps. It's essentially a command point in the middle of the map that you can take control of, and it would show blue if the other team took it. These kind of features can be a secondary points-scoring feature in some maps, or be otherwise utilized depending on the server.

Roles are almost as important as knowing maps in CTF. Typical roles are attacker, mid player and defender, and you should choose one and focus on it. Attackers go after flags, defenders stay at base to protect their own flag, and mid players hang out in the middle to help teammates bringing the enemy's flag back, kill enemies trying to make off with the mid player's flag, and generally harass the other team and provide support for your own. You can switch between these a little, but it's best to pick one and stay at it.

Knowing the powers and features of the game is very server-specific, but essentially it just means that you should use every feature you have at your disposal to your advantage. If you've got a special donor perk or a powerup, learn how to use it and make sure you do actually use it!

83

💡 TIPS FOR PROS:

- Sneak attacks on the flag are good, especially if you can catch the other team with an empty flag room!

- On the other hand, attacking with a big group is also super effective. Overwhelm the enemy with a big group, and in the chaos, steal their flag!

- Typically you don't want to run across the most obvious part of the map with the flag. Try to find secret back passages and tunnels to get back. When trying to track down your own flag, realize that other players will do this as well, so check the same passages (and always be ready for a fight when on your own).

- Communicate with your team. Use the chat to let them know where the enemy is, where the flag is, that you need help defending etc. This is often massively overlooked, but it is essential for really performing well at this minigame.

Note the player in the chat discussing strategy. Working together on a plan is always helpful in a game like CTF.

Cops and Crims

Basic idea: A simulation of the squad-based first-person shooter *Counter-Strike* in Minecraft, Cops and Crims involves short matches of shooter combat where one team is either trying to either kill the other team and/or set off a bomb before it's defused, and the other team is trying to also kill the other team and/or keep the bomb from going off.

Number of players: Typically no more than 16

How long does it take: Rounds are just a few minutes long, but usually each team gets three or so chances to play each side, which can take around 15-20 minutes.

How hard is it: Fairly simple, unless playing against people who know the maps very well. Then it becomes something more like real *Counter-Strike*, which is a game with a high skill ceiling.

Where can it be found: mc.hypixel.net

⚙ IMPORTANT FEATURES:

Anyone who's ever played *Counter-Strike* or *Counter-Strike: GO* will find Cops and Crims immediately familiar, and that's because it's a pretty awesomely accurate recreation of that game inside of Minecraft. It comes complete with guns and a gun store at the beginning of each match (can also buy grenades, armor etc.), as well as highly detailed recreations of *Counter-Strike* levels. Each map has "bomb sites" where the crims team needs to place the bomb (only one site needs to have the bomb of the two) and where the cops need to defend.

When the bomb is placed (one random player on the crims team has the bomb each time), the cops need to go try to defuse it. This is where the game gets a little different from CS, as you actually have to snip all of the red wires in a big grid that will pop up on the screen. Do it fast enough, and you'll defuse the bomb and win. Don't get red wires you need, though, and your cop butt is gonna be blown sky-high.

Basic Strategy for Winning: Like in real *Counter-Strike,* the keys to winning Cops and Crims matches are to know the levels VERY well, work as a team, and buy the right gear.

Counter-Strike levels are famous for being very well designed (for the most part), and pro CS teams often win because of their knowledge of very specific places to sit on the map and wait to shoot other players. While the Minecraft version isn't going to work exactly the same way as the real one, choke points and hiding places are still important, and many of them are the same between the two. Learn these for each map to become unstoppable.

Working as a team is also key. You have a very specific goal, not much time to accomplish it, and not very many players to do it with. If you spread out and just do your own thing, more than likely you're going to get picked off one by one, or you'll end up with not enough players to take on what's left of the other team. It's even worse if they're organized and you're not, so communicate, stick together, and you'll do much better overall.

Gearing the right way is super important in Cops and Crims, meaning that you should spend your money at the beginning of each match on the right stuff. Partly it comes down to personal style (shotgun vs. machine gun etc.), but you almost always want to buy at least some armor, one grenade, and a better weapon. Many people swear by the carbines, but you should try them all and learn what you like the best.

The red spray-painted arrows in Cops and Crims point the way to bombsites, which are key to winning from either side of the game.

💡 TIPS FOR PROS:

· Holding the sneak key will make your gun go to single-shot mode, which is more accurate.

· Guns have recoil, so you often need to aim lower than you think to hit people.

· Grenades won't hurt teammates, but they can hurt you, and if they do hit a teammate while flying, they'll go off immediately. So, be realllllly careful with grenades!

Duels

This duel features enchanted Swords and pretty decent armor. This means that it takes a lot to kill someone, and that getting critical hits by attacking during a jump can be very important to winning.

Basic idea: A very simple 1 v 1 arena combat game where there is a modifier/powerup for each match.

Number of players: 2

How long does it take: Less than 2 minutes, usually

How hard is it: Simple to play, but you'll need to be good at PVP combat to win.

Where can it be found: us.lichcraft.com

⚙ IMPORTANT FEATURES:

Testing your PVP mettle in massive brawls with a lot of other players is fun, but it doesn't necessarily tell you who is the best at PVP, because there are so many other players hitting each other and you at once.

Duels, on the other hand, is a minigame that settles the score once and for all by only allowing two players into a match, where they have to use all of their combat skills to slay the other and come out as the undisputed winner.

These matches are regular Minecraft combat, except with one twist every game in the form of some sort of modifier. This can be that players are using Bows, Swords with amplified damage, or a number of other modifiers, and you can choose which you want to play with when you create the match (or choose an existing match with a modifier you like).

The arenas are simple and don't have much in the way of strategic features, so it really is all about the combat in this one.

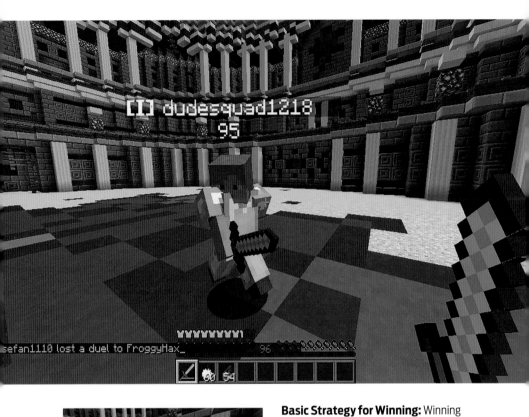

Learning good overall PVP skills is essential to any duel.

Basic Strategy for Winning: Winning Duels comes down to being good at Minecraft combat. You need to know things like how to jitter-click (left clicking then right clicking then left clicking again over and over with a Sword so that you hit then block then hit), how to get critical hits (attack while jumping) and how to strafe, circle, and perform other Minecraft combat tactics. It's also good to know what modifier your duel will have and to be decent at that particular style of combat.

A duelist enters the arena, prepared to take down the foe or die trying.

💡 TIPS FOR PROS:

- Really, the main tip is to practice combat! Get good at killing mobs in survival mode, do a lot of PVP in other minigames, and then take those skills to Duels.

Paintball

Paintball is pretty chaotic, but it's super fun for its speed.

Basic idea: Use Snowballs as "paintballs," shooting them at players from another team which will be "out" and have to respawn if they're hit once. There are also powerups on some servers, and the overall goal is for teams try to reach a certain score or have the highest score of hits over a certain amount of time.

Number of players: ~24

How long does it take: Usually around five minutes

How hard is it: Easy to throw Snowballs, but learning to get kills and stay alive takes some getting used to

Where can it be found: mc.hypixel.net is definitely the biggest one, but it can be found on a lot of other smaller servers

You were fragged by oleeskild
noob_with_dirt activated Triple Shot
metalmauro10 activated Nuke
NUCLEAR MISSILE INBOUND!
mpact in 5

⚙ IMPORTANT FEATURES:

If survival minigames seem like a little too much commitment and effort
for your Minecrafting session, and some of these other PVP games take a bit too much skill
(some of those players are goooood), Paintball is on the opposite side of the spectrum of
minigames in that it's quick, easy, and doesn't require much knowledge of the ins and outs of
Minecraft.

Paintball is pretty easy to pick up: all you do is run around a map trying
to hit players with "paintballs," which are actually just Snowballs under
a different name. If you hit a player once, they are immediately warped back to spawn and
you and your team gets points. The first team to get
a certain amount of points or the team with the most points after a set amount of time
wins. On some servers getting "kills" earns you coins that you can use to purchase powerups
for either you or your team, like a triple-shot or reducing the amount of deaths your team
has.

And that's it! Pretty simple, no? Don't be fooled though; while picking up a game of Paintball
is easy and you're probably going to get at least a few kills in every match you play, there are
some players that have taken this little minigame rather seriously and can hit other players
with ease from far across the map. With practice, though, you can become one of these

Two blue-team players await the white team onslaught and start shooting paintballs in the direction they think it's coming.

skillshot aficionados and start to get your name in the Top 3 of the scoresheet with regularity.

Basic Strategy for Winning: Different servers have different versions of this game, but across each you'll need to learn to throw the Paintballs very accurately and to be very good at ambushing other players. It's pretty easy to get hit in this game, and getting killed a few times isn't bad, but you want to try and attack players when they can't see you as much as possible, because your deaths will add up (and so will theirs).

You can practice throwing Snowballs on creative mode in single player to get a bit of a better idea of how to shoot Paintballs, but really, playing a lot is what will get you better at this part of the game.

Learning to strafe is very useful in Paintball, because any target that can be tracked easily will also be hit with ease.

Some servers (like Hypixel) also have powerups you can unlock by getting kills or by spending server money and experience, so make sure you take a look at those. Focus on one particular powerup if possible and get really good at it so that you become experienced and effective.

💡 TIPS FOR PROS:

- On Hypixel, Strongarm and Tripleshot are two of the most powerful powerups, so try those out if you get some kills and have some money to spend.

- Stay moving. Most players don't have great aim and will spray a line of Snowballs at any player they see, and if you're standing still, you have a lot greater of a chance to get hit.

SMASH

Smash arenas look similar to Skywars, with their many hanging platforms and places where you can easily drop to your death.

Basic idea: A Minecraft version of the ever-popular *Super Smash Bros.* video game, involving players in an arena punching each other in an attempt to knock the other players off. Powerups, weapons, and other items will spawn around the arena.

Number of players: As few as 4 and up to 50, but generally around 6-12

How long does it take: Around 2-5 minutes

How hard is it: Like real *Smash Bros.*, it's pretty wild and a lot of it is up to chance (such as what powerups you get), but it doesn't take too long to learn the basics

Where can it be found: us.shotbow.net, us.mineplex.com, mineca.de, many other versions out there under different names

⚙ IMPORTANT FEATURES:

Super Smash Bros. is one of Nintendo's flagship video game franchises because of its frenetic competitive gameplay that's very easy to pick up, but which can also be played with a lot of skill if the player is willing to put in the time. People absolutely love the weapons, powerups and quick, wild matches, and that energy and excitement are what you'll find with the many different *Super Smash Bros.* Minecraft recreations out there.

The premise is exactly the same as with the real game, though minus the unique heroes; players can punch and "ground pound" (smash from a jump) other players and give them damage, as well as pick up items that randomly spawn around the map to use.

These items include everything from super OP weapons like The Smasher (does damage to blocks and 200 to any player nearby) to traps you can throw like the Monster Egg (spawns a mob that will fight other players for you). There are also boosts like speed and health potions, all of which combine to make for a game that will be different each time you play.

Being very aware of where other players are is of utmost importance in Smash.

Basic Strategy for Winning: Smash strategy is mostly about getting and using items (and hoping for the best ones) and attacking at the right time. Like in other PVP and competitive Minecraft, letting other players take each other out is always a good idea in Smash, and you typically only want to go one-on-one with another player instead of involving yourself in big brawls. It's also a good idea to use your regular attacks often, especially the jump smash (jump up and then push the sneak key), and don't make big attacks on other players until you have a good weapon. Learning the different weapons and items is also key, so, as always, practice makes perfect.

One thing you definitely don't want in Smash, or any PVP, is to catch on fire. If you ever see anyone dropping Fire Charges or the like, just stay away. The damage you will take before it goes out will be tremendous.

💡 TIPS FOR PROS:

· Don't forget the ground pound/jump smash! Most players do, and that's a mistake because it's very powerful.

· Avoid the edges. This is really just good advice for most minigames, but especially in Smash.

· Hold on to grenades and traps until you are pretty sure you can hit a player.

· You can double-jump, and you should use this to try and jump back up onto the arena if you fall off.

Spleef

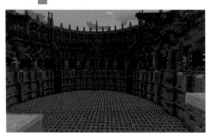

A traditional Spleef arena, but with the twist of using TNT instead of Wool (boom!).

Basic idea: An arena has a floor of blocks that can be destroyed with a weapon of some sort. Players try to knock the floor out from beneath other players to make them fall, and the last one that hasn't fallen to their doom wins.

Number of players: 2 or more, up to around 24

How long does it take: Less than 5 minutes

How hard is it: Very easy to play, but winning can be random

Where can it be found: All over! Almost every big server (especially those with an arcade) has some version of Spleef.

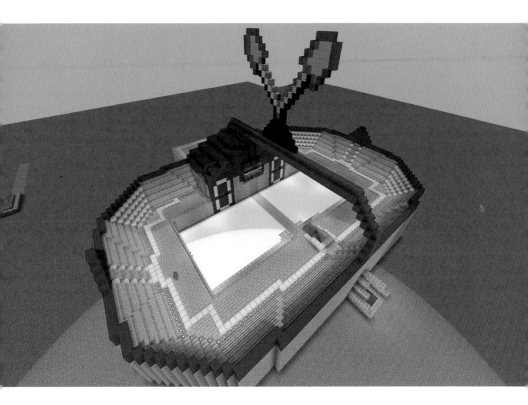

⚙ IMPORTANT FEATURES:

The original big-time minigame; the one that started the trend of making minigames! Spleef isn't quite as popular on some big servers as it once was, but this is the minigame that many of us think of as the official Minecraft minigame, and it's still just as fun to play as it ever was.

The concept is all about the set up, and it's pretty simple: a one-block-thick layer of Wool or another material sits above a pool of Lava or a chasm in an arena constructed of unbreakable materials. Players start on top of the layer of Wool in the corners of the arena and use Flint and Tinder, Fire Charges, Eggs, a Bow, or another weapon to destroy the Wool in the path of the other players in the match. When the Wool disappears it leaves gaps in the floor through which players can fall. The last player who has avoided falling wins!

There are endless awesome variants on this game, including having permanent blocks to jump to for safety, incorporating a maze into the arena, adding Ender Pearls to the mix (to teleport around the playing field), using multiple layers of Wool (either directly under the first or on a second level below) or even putting blocks of TNT here and there to mix things up a bit, all of which are a lot of fun.

Spatial awareness will win you Spleef matches. Watch where the edges are and where other players are, or things could go badly pretty fast.

Spleef arenas have become so popular that they're pretty much a genre of structure in Minecraft, and you can find Spleef maps on some servers or on PlanetMinecraft.com to download. Or, you can make your own version!

Basic Strategy for Winning: Spleef is more about fun and craziness than strategy, but if there is any tactic that will help you, it's to watch your feet and keep moving. Standing still makes you a target for other players you might not see (behind or underneath you in multi-layered Spleef), but make sure you know you're running toward solid ground.

You can also work on your weapon accuracy to get better at taking out other players. Playing with infinite ammo in creative mode single player is always helpful, and will help you in other minigames as well.

💡 TIPS FOR PROS

Once you die in Spleef, you'll get to spectate the match and fly around watching the players who bested you take each other on.

- Watch around you in all directions. People love to sneak attack in Spleef.

- Try to cut other players off by surrounding them with dropped blocks. The less space they have to move in, the more likely they are to fall.

- Don't get cut off yourself! If you notice the area you're in is being riddled with holes, try to get to a more solid area where you can move easier with less danger of falling.

Warlords

A Warlords player runs toward the fray.

Basic idea: RPG fantasy-like PVP combat, complete with classes, crazy weapons, spells and powers. Comes in capture the flag, team deathmatch and domination (control point capture) styles of play.

How long does it take: Around 10-20 minutes a match

How hard is it: You can definitely run around smacking people within seconds, but actually learning the classes and when and how to use spells and powers is very complex

Where can it be found: mc.hypixel.net

⚙ IMPORTANT FEATURES:

If you're looking for one of the most visually and conceptually awesome minigames on the planet, you might want to give the thrilling Warlords minigame on Hypixel a try. Going for and achieving a fully-realized fantasy aesthetic, Hypixel uses custom-made, gorgeous textures and items that automatically load to make characters look like fantasy warriors, wizards and more, with epic armor and giant weapons to boot.

Before joining a match, you'll want to check out the different classes and chose one. Each one not only has a different look, but also entirely different weapons and spells. Essentially, each class gives you a role on your team.

Other features in this minigame include having a horse, being able to purchase and upgrade your various stats for your player (such as damage done), being able to eventually purchase class specializations (more and better powers), being able to craft, repair and upgrade weapons, and taking quests that will give you more experience to spend on the upgrades in the minigame. It really is a full-featured minigame, and it's one of the best in this book or anywhere online.

Basic Strategy for Winning: The basics of the three different types of play in this minigame (team deathmatch, CTF, and domination) are the same as they would be in other games, so basic strategy is to apply the specifics of Warlords to these games.

For the most part, that involves playing your class right. If you are a Warrior, for example, you'll be a front-line brawler and should just charge right in and start hitting people with sharp things (this is a good class for starting out at Warlords). Mages, on the other hand, will want to stay back and shoot spells at people from a distance, the Paladin is a bit of a warrior/healer/buffer who can make the battle easier for friends and worse for enemies, and the Shaman is another kind of distance magic-user that also has some healing and buffing. Learn how each class works by playing some of each, and then pick one and stick to it.

This sticking to it is important, because the other very important part of Warlords is to level up your character and weapons. This game is very cumulative, so when you first start, you'll be playing with some players that are much, much stronger than you. Do as well as you can, and finish the match so that you can then spend your earned experience on leveling up your character. Keep doing this, and eventually you'll be one of the strongest characters in any match, able to turn the tide of the whole thing for your team.

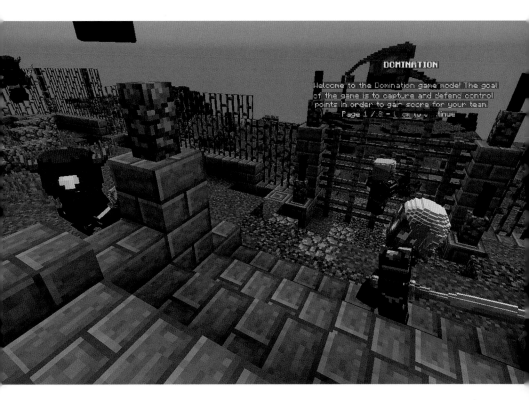

💡 TIPS FOR PROS

· Communication and organization can turn this game from a chaotic frenzy into a real competition, or it can help you overrun a team that isn't communicating. Give people roles, play your class the way it should be, and you will find the game to be much more strategic and less insane.

· Learn the maps! We say this all the time in this book, but it's oh so important in minigames like Warlords where you need to get to specific places (like where the flag or domination points are) very quickly. This is less important in team deathmatch, but it'll never hurt you to know the maps.

· Use your experience points wisely. If you're not sure how to do that, ask another player or use the forums.

TNT Wizards

Choose your class in TNT Wizards through the inventory. It'll give a short description of each, and you can choose any of them you like (there aren't locked ones like most Kit PVP).

Basic idea: A domination-style PVP game where each player picks a class of wizard and has access to dangerous spells to use against each other (and the landscape).

Number of players: Up to 20

How long does it take: ~10 minutes

How hard is it: One of the easier class-based PVP games to get into

Where can it be found: mc.hypixel.net

⚙ IMPORTANT FEATURES:

Who doesn't want to be a wizard? We know we're into the idea of wrathfully slingin' the powers of magic at our foes, and that's why we love the Wizards minigame. This one is a simple PVP "capture the command point" mode that has each player pick a team and a kit, and each kit is a different type of wizard with a variety of unique powers.

The powers and wizard-types run the gamut from fireball throwers to ice wizards and more, and each class typically has an exploding spell attack that has a special feature to it, like a fireball that burns enemies (a Fire Charge shot when a staff is used), and a special defensive power, like an instant teleport. Most powers take "mana," which in this case is the icons in your hunger bar, which are used up quickly but also regenerate very quickly.

The matches themselves are set in an arena that is decently sized and typically contains all destructible blocks, which makes Wizards somewhat unique to PVP matches, which often feature indestructible arenas. Wizards arenas are like this because the powers at the disposal of each wizard in the match are mighty forces of nature that tend to explode and cause area damage, and part of the fun of Wizards matches is that the explosions wreck the environment as the match goes along. And, since the gravity is much lower in Wizards matches, you can jump just about anywhere, making every block in the arena part of the battleground. By the time a winner is announced, the whole arena will be in glorious ruins.

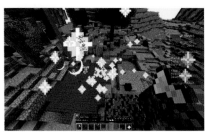

You'll often find yourself in this position in Wizards, both because you automatically can jump quite high and because things will be blowing up pretty much nonstop.

Points rack up for a team based on the amount of time a command point has been owned by that team, and when one team reaches 2,000 points, they win this mighty struggle of magic users.

Wizards is as chaotic as it gets, but its balance of excellent unique classes, destructible terrain, low gravity, heavily armored players, and the PVP + command points structure makes for one of the best PVP experiences in the world of Minecraft.

Basic Strategy for Winning: The combat in Wizards is a little different from many such fast-paced PVP minigames, as although your spells have spectacular effects and do damage in an area, each wizard is actually pretty tough to kill and will not go down without more than a couple direct hits.

A player attempts to get on a heavily bombarded capture point.

Additionally, you aren't just trying to kill your enemies; you're also trying to walk on two different command points so that you capture them for your team. If enemy players are on the command point, they will start capturing it for their team instead, and the more players from one team on the command point, the more likely it is to go to that team. Once it's been captured, the other team has to keep enemy players off of it to capture it back; otherwise it will keep going fully back to the team that last captured it.

Working with your team is of particular importance in Wizards, and the team that does this the best is much more likely to keep control of the domination points.

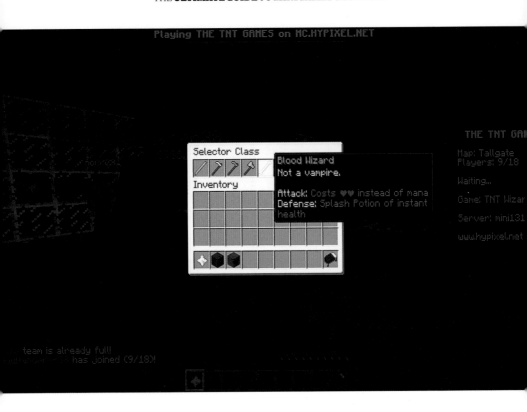

You can see capture points from a distance because of the team-colored "beacon" coming out of them, which is helpful both for navigation and for knowing who controls what point.

ᗄ TIPS FOR PROS

· Select your Wizard class before each match, or you can let it assign you one automatically. Try a few different ones in your first few games, and use the one whose powers you like the most.

· Once you've selected your wizard-type, it's locked in for the rest of the match, so make sure to try a few out and find one you're good with.

BLUE wins in 04:45

Alpha: RED
Beta: BLUE
Gamma: RED in 4s

Kills: 2
Assists: 0
Deaths: 2

www.hypixel.net

HERE'S THE LIST OF WIZARDS CLASSES AND THEIR POWERS

FIRE WIZARD
Attack Power: Launches a fireball
Defense Power: Instant teleportation

KINETIC WIZARD
Attack Power: High damage, short-range railgun
Defense Power: Gravity gun

ICE WIZARD
Attack Power: Freeze shot to slow enemies
Defense Power: Puts up a wall of Ice

WITHER WIZARD
Attack Power: Exploding extra-poisonous Wither skull shot
Defense Power: An extra row of "absorption hearts"

BLOOD WIZARD
Attack Power: Normal attack costs 2 hearts instead of mana
Defense Power: Has a Splash Potion that instantly regenerates health

115

Skyblock
& Variants

Skyblock minigames are one of the pillars of the minigame community in Minecraft. They're tough, competitive and require a lot of knowledge of Minecraft, including everything from how to build, to how the physics works, to how to farm and (on most versions) how to be a serious OP warrior in combat.

Skyblock games have a lot of variation among them, but there's one thing that they always contain: you, the player, spawning on a small island floating in the air. In regular Skyblock, you'll have to use limited resources to overcome challenges and possibly even fight other players, while in variants like Skywars, you'll be focusing a lot more on combat than on building or gathering resources.

Skyblock matches are a way to show that you really do know a lot about this game, and learning how to dominate in competitive matches is a sure way to get respect from other players. Take these tips, play like a pro, and become one of the top players on your favorite server.

Skyblock

Basic idea: You (and sometimes others) spawn on a small piece of land hanging in the air with very few items or resources. You have to use what you have to create more resources and land, and you usually have to compete with and kill other teams doing the same thing to win.

Number of players: 1-12ish

How long does it take: If people are good at it (and you're playing competitively), not as long as you think (~10 minutes, less sometimes). If people are new at it or it's not competitive, or on servers where not many items are given to you at the beginning, this can go on for any number of hours. Agrarian Skies in particular can take far over 50 hours to complete!

How hard is it: Very! You really have to know your Minecraft stuff.

Where can it be found: Pretty much everywhere! Here are some top places to check it out: skyblock.net, play.gotpvp.com, mc.desiredcraft.net, yaymc.com, play.mythcraftpvp.com, us.mineplex.com, play.primemc.org, mc-central.net, fadecloud.com, play.omegarealm.com, minetime.com, play.guildcraf.org, and play.skybattle.net.

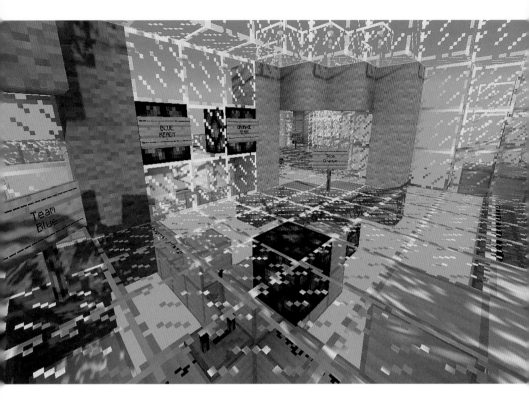

⚙ IMPORTANT FEATURES:

Skyblock is one of the more challenging ways to play Minecraft, and it is so much fun. It'll actually help you learn quite a lot about the game and its rules, and it can help give you ideas for regular play that you might not have had otherwise.

Skyblock involves you (or you and teammates) spawning on an island floating in the sky that is made of very few blocks. Usually it has a little Dirt, a tree (or just Saplings) and some Water and a Chest with a few items in it. What's in the Chest and what's on the island differ with various versions of the map (of which there are many), but the goal is almost always one of two things. One—you complete various tasks by creatively and efficiently using the items and blocks at your disposal, such as create 20 Cobblestone or gather 6 Wool, while staying alive (usually you only have one to three lives). Or two— in competitive Skyblock, you want to kill the other players, who have their own Skyblocks nearby, and be the last player or team standing.

Basic Strategy for Winning: Skyblock is intensely challenging because you have to be pretty knowledgeable about the rules of Minecraft in order to turn the few blocks and resources at your disposal into more things. For instance, if you do not start with any Cobblestone, you need to know how to make a Cobblestone generator out of Lava and Water. Or, in another example, you may need to build out a platform away from your island in order to let mobs spawn on it.

As we mentioned, there are many variations on this game, and you may find one server's version to be very different from another's. We'd suggest downloading either the SwipeShotTeam's Skyblock Warriors map (bit.ly/skyblockwarriorsmap) for an easy intro or, for those looking for a true challenge (and an intro into a bunch of great mods!), the incredible Agrarian Skies (downloadable through Feed the Beast mod loader found here: www.feed-the-beast.com).

One of the primary things across most Skyblock games is that there will be a series of challenges to complete that will give you items as rewards for completing them. These are essential to continuing to play, so definitely do the challenges. On PVP Skyblock, there may or may not be challenges, but in regular Skyblock there almost always are.

♀ TIPS FOR PROS:
- **Be very careful with resources.** You only have so much of everything (that's the point of Skyblock), so if you don't know how to do something, or are worried you might get it wrong (like a Cobble generator or farming trees for Saplings), don't risk it: look it up or ask for help. If you somehow destroy all of your Leaves and Saplings, all of your Dirt, Sand, ways to get seeds, or your Bucket, you're going to be unable to go much farther and will have to start a new Skyblock.

· Learn how to create different Cobblestone generators. These are very useful and necessary in Skyblock, but are also helpful in regular Minecraft. The simplest Cobble generator involves digging a 4 block long pit that's 1 block deep, except that it should be 2 blocks deep on the second block from the left. Then you put Lava in the far right square of the pit (4 from the left) and very quickly put a Bucket of Water in the block in the far left. This should flow toward the Lava, and there should be a block of Cobblestone created where they hit (in the third block from the left, one to the right of the 2 deep part). You can keep mining this Cobblestone out, and more will appear each time due to the way that Water and Lava work to generate Cobble.

· Create a second level of your Skyblock island by dropping a column of Water off the side or through a hole in your first island. Fall through this a bit, dropping blocks in a column as you go. Make sure you don't fall out or too far! When you create a column far enough down for your liking, start placing blocks perpendicular to your column that you can stand on. Expand this area into a platform, and you have a second level to work with.

· Keep your green-covered dirt blocks and let them grow Grass that you can then punch and break to get Seeds. These are super important, because farming is how you're gonna get most of your food in early Skyblock.

- When you have enough blocks to create more platforms, create a dark room or a platform with a Gate or Door (to keep mobs from crawling over to you!) far from your original platform. Let hostile mobs spawn there so that you can kill them and harvest their goodies. Be careful that you create this in a way that it's easy to kill the mobs without getting killed yourself, or make it so that it's a true mob grinder if you have the right stuff (Cactus works great, but it's not that easy to do that).

- To farm friendly mobs like Sheep and Cows, you need to get them to spawn. Another platform should be created at least 24 blocks away from the edge of the rest of your base, and it should have a Grass floor and nothing covering the roof. You need it to be this far away, have Grass at the bottom, and at least level 9 light (fairly bright) to get friendly mobs to spawn. This will happen naturally during the day, but you can also light it up super well with Torches if you want to speed up the process.

SkyWars

Server
SkyWars 2

Coins
7

Class
None

Players
8/16

MINECA.DE

JWFireWing

...t in minutes and ...sec... in minutes... start of the game.

ew! rip chicken bannanna's ping is too good

Skywars Variant

Basic idea: Start on a floating island like Skyblock, but with more initial items, fewer resources to exploit, and more of a PVP focus.

Number of players: Depends on the server, but needs at least 3 to be fun. Can go up to dozens though!

How long does it take: Usually takes at least five minutes, but can go as long as it takes for the really good players to duke it out (so up to half an hour is rare, but not out of the question).

How hard is it: Easier than Skyblock, harder than regular PVP. Good players have strategy on lockdown for this game, so it can be very hard to win against more experienced players.

Where can it be found: mc.hypixel.net, fadecloud.com, play.gotpvp.com, play.guildcraft.com, play.thedestinymc.com, us.mineplex.com, and many others

⚙ IMPORTANT FEATURES:

Skywars is based on Skyblock, but instead of having small spaces for each player/team and having a focus on building and creating resources, each player in Skywars has a hollow island with Chests with goods inside and much fewer resources to mine. The point in Skywars is more about combat and making a PVP Skyblock type game much faster, and it's a lot of crazy fun to play.

Basic Strategy for Winning: One important factor in Skywars is your Chest(s) in your island. All sorts of different types of items and armor can spawn there, and you will likely get at least something to kill people with. You'll need to get down to your Chest and equip items very quickly, because other players will be trying to do the same to get the jump on you.

The next step is usually to collect some blocks from your island to use to create a bridge over to another island. This is how the combat works in Skywars—one player usually sneaks over to another's island and attempts an ambush, then combat ensues. You can also try sniping from a distance if you have a Bow or any other distance weapon (depending on what items and mods are being used on the server you're playing on), but you need to be pretty good at aiming to do this for very long.

Getting another player's items is very important to becoming powerful enough to win this game, but don't hesitate to kill people by knocking them off the islands if you get a chance. A kill's a kill, and one less enemy is always good.

💡 TIPS FOR PROS:

· The island in the middle of the Skywars arena has very good items in it, so one strategy is to ignore other players when possible and go for the center. This takes some skilled bridging, and it leaves you vulnerable to attack, so be careful when rushing the center.

· Bows aren't the only good projectile weapon! Eggs and snowballs will knock players back, which you can use to make them fall to their deaths. Use these when you get them!

· Build walls (barricades) around the part of your island you're hanging out on when things have settled down after the first few minutes. These will allow you to avoid being seen as well as avoid projectiles. If you create a few little windows, you can also shoot out at other players with much less danger.

- Use sneaking/crouching to build your bridges so that you don't fall. This is absolutely key to building fast bridges, which itself is key to winning Skywars. If you have time, it's a good idea not to do just a 1 block wide bridge, but instead to put a wall on one or both sides at least 1 block high. This is because players will often try to shoot things at you to knock you off your bridges.

- Check your Furnace, too. There may be other useful items in there!

- Enderpearls appear in many Skywars games, and they're one of the most useful ways to get around the arena. You can even use them to get to the center faster if you're careful.

- Many servers allow you to use kits and/or buy items from their shop with server money that you can use in the game. These will change your whole game, but make sure you buy useful things like weapons, armor, TNT, etc. However, note that if you're way overpowered, the game won't really be competitive or fun, and other players will get pretty frustrated with you.

Other Variants

A Skywars player bides his time waiting for the enemy to come to him.

As one of the premier minigames for Minecraft, people are creating all sorts of other variants for Skyblock all the time. Whether it's taking basic Skyblock and adding new kits or items, changing the initial set-up or creating new challenges for people, or whether it's making a much different game that also uses floating islands as its core feature, you'll find a lot of options out there to play! For instance, SkyGrid is a variant that has a giant grid of single blocks floating next to each other, which you'll have to collect and gather together (the single blocks can be just about any block or item in the game), while SkyWalls is a combination of The Walls and Skyblock.

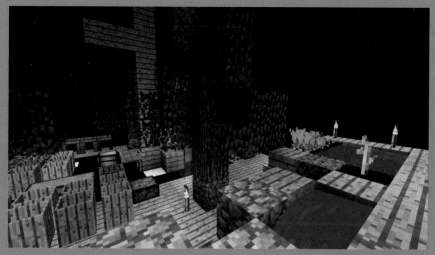

Agrarian Skies is chock full of some of the most popular mods that add new items and systems to your game. In just this shot alone you see new Barrels, a new type of Chest, a Half-Slab Furnace, and a Sifting Table, used to get mineral materials and more from Dirt, Gravel, Sand, and Dust (Dust!) blocks.

Skyblock Mod Spotlight:
Agrarian Skies

www.feed-the-beast.com

Mods are awesome: that, we think most everyone would agree on. However, since mods add so much new stuff and change up the game so extensively, it can be super overwhelming to fire one up and see all this new stuff you don't know how to mess with. Many mods come with little in-game Books that you can open up and read, but trying to remember all the things you read and switching back and forth between them and actually playing is pretty darn hard, even for the best Crafters.

That's why we suggest that, if you're looking to actually learn how to do some of the amazing things in mods like all of the Tinkers' mods, Thaumcraft, Thermal Expansion, or Applied Energistics, check out the Agrarian Skies modpack. Actually a super, super modded version of Skyblock and available on the FTB Launcher, Agrarian Skies puts you in a world where you have very little to start with, but all of the things you need to eventually build everything in the mods. It uses a very well-done and inventive questing system to teach you how to do a ton of the stuff in these mods by making them goals, and it does so in a way that's both hugely entertaining and also quite challenging. If we had to pick, Agrarian Skies would be our very favorite modpack of all.

Long-Form
Minigames

Not all minigames are short-lived bouts of competitive fun. No—while the quick minigame that begins, is fought, and ends in mere minutes is fun and appealing, there are those Crafters out there that seek more from online play. They look to battle others in earnest, to use their hard-won Minecraft skills in direct competition with others from all over the world. To really pit what they know about the game against other humans, and to have it be exciting.

Those looking for this kind of competition have created a strong segment of the Minecraft minigame universe to have exactly these kinds of competitions. These are the long-form minigames, and they are some hard, difficult, super-rewarding ways to play Minecraft.

Each of these games is its own approach to a long-term way to play online multiplayer Minecraft, but what you can know about each right now is that they take dedication, thought and just about every possible bit of knowledge about Minecraft that you could muster to do well at.

For those that dig the complexity and cumulative nature of MMOs, or those that want to really show what they're made of when it comes to making a mark in the ground in Minecraft over days, weeks, months, and even years (instead of doing so very quickly, as most minigames require), long-form multiplayer minigames will be the version of this video game that you will love the most.

Of those available, the best so far are Factions, MineZ and MineZ 2, Prison, and Cops and Robbers.

Factions

Basic idea: Players join "factions" that claim chunks of land in a randomly generated Minecraft world. Factions recruit players, gather resources, and battle other factions, trying to kill them and thus cause their claimed areas to become accessible (and thus lootable!).

Number of players: Any. Factions servers are huge and can have just a few players or thousands.

How long does it take: It doesn't end! The wars go on until the server is reset or goes offline.

How hard is it: It's not hard at all to start a faction and build something in some claimed land, but fighting other factions can be very hard.

Where can it be found: pvp.origin.org, play.gotpvp.com, mc.deseiredcraft.net, pvp.desteria.com, play.primemc.org, mc-central.net, mc.arkhamnetwork.org, na.badlion.com, play.guildcraft.org, us.lichcraft.com, and many, many others

⚙ IMPORTANT FEATURES:

Factions is among the most popular Minecraft minigames, and it's also one of the most in-depth when it comes to what you can do. The basic idea is that you are in a regular Survival world with many other players (typically there's no limit to the amount), but you have the added ability to join a faction.

Factions are essentially teams of players that can claim a "chunk" of land for their faction. Only players that are members of the faction can open chests or build or destroy anything by hand on a faction's land. Non-members will find themselves unable to affect another faction's land, except by using TNT, Lava, or Water dropped onto it. Typically, you can't be hurt on your faction's claimed land, as well.

Playing Factions is best done with friends, whether those you know in the real world or those met online, because a one-person faction can't get much done. Find a faction to join, or get some buddies together to make one of your own!

Land chunks extend from the bedrock to sky and can claimed by using Power, which each player has in a certain amount, and some of which is lost when the player dies. Usually a player starts with 10 Power, claims land using 1 Power and loses 3 Power on death, but this can be different between servers.

When a player joins a faction, their Power is added to the faction total, allowing the faction to claim more land. Be warned though: when you lose Power from dying, that Power will be subtracted from your faction's total. If your faction ever has less power than it has claimed chunks of land, you can start to lose that land. Over time, your Power can grow back, thankfully, but this happens very, very slowly.

The goal of Factions is to grow your faction, get more money (used to buy items and/or land), recruit new faction members, and declare war against or ally up with other factions. So basically, it turns (almost) vanilla Minecraft into an all out tribal war. It's a never-ending brutal war for domination and land, and it's one heck of a cool way to compete in Minecraft over an extended period of time.

Basic Strategy for Winning: There's no real "winner" in Factions, as new people can usually join and create new factions all the time, but Factions is a whole lot of fun to play over time, as you'll become very attached to your base and group. Things will change on the server, big attacks will happen and get talked about, and all sorts of other drama and action can occur. That being said, there are some things that are good ideas when playing a Factions game:

POWER:

Power is the essential resource in Factions that makes the game run. Each player has their own power from -10 to 10 total. Each faction adds every faction member's power on to the faction's total, whether that number is negative or positive. A faction can only claim as many chunks of land as that faction has power. Power is reduced when you're killed when not in a "warzone" (someplace designated for fighting, like a PVP zone), and power only rebuilds by being online, which it does at a slow pace. Any pieces of land lost to losing power will have to be reclaimed, and whatever you have on those chunks will be available for other players to take/trash/utterly destroy with no mercy, and if anyone sees your spot, that's exactly what'll happen.

- If you're creating your own faction, get some friends to join, or ask in the general chat if anyone needs a faction. A single-player faction can't claim very much land, and what you can grab will get wiped out pretty darn fast. The more people you have, the more land you can take, and the more of a buffer you have when it comes to losing power (if your 3 player faction claims 20 chunks of land, you can have a total of 10 deaths before you start losing chunks).

Kiingtong
100 % Health

idcontal Jandomines: i need a place tomake 'the ro
lified [Hero] ryanjosh: bayani! why

33

16   63

· Get VERY far from spawn to claim land for your faction. If you create a faction base within even 5,000 squares from spawn, people will find it. At least 8,000 squares in two directions is smart, and even farther is better. Also, don't go an equal distance in two directions from spawn. Go a little farther on one axis (use your in-game location counter to tell your coordinates) than the other, because many people like to use coordinates with equal numbers as meeting points.

· Leave **absolutely no gaps** in your faction walls. This means that any part of your base you build should be fully within your faction's claimed land. This is because players that aren't in your faction (aka, those dudes you don't want in your base) can't open Doors, push Levers or Buttons, break blocks or build within the land claimed by your faction. They can walk through your land though, meaning they can create gaps in your base anywhere that you haven't claimed all of the land the base is on, and then they can walk into your base, see what you have going on, find weak points and decide how to attack you and get your things. Trust us, this will happen. **Some might think this wouldn't happen, because it takes work and knowledge, but it will. Players are that good and that committed. If you don't believe it, try building your faction base close to spawn. Even if your stuff survives (it won't), you'll quickly see how hard people will work to mess your stuff up.**

n't have enough power to claim that land.
eyMen
action already owns this land.
] ×·Minecrafters [King]angusg16: I love facs now :P
h: Benbennett1 is auctioning 83×Coal for $50. Type /auc
h: Auction for 83×Coal ends in 10 seconds!
h: Auction for 83×Coal ends in 3 seconds!
h: Auction for 83×Coal ended with no bids.
h: Benbennett1 is auctioning 1×Human Head for $100.
/auc
tte] Place a sign headed [Private] next to a chest to
ryCrates] A Mystery Crate has spawned at -6235, 63,
]!
] +LunaGuild [Default]Captin5okz: mystery crate
h: Auction for 1×Human Head ends in 10 seconds!
h: Auction for 1×Human Head ends in 3 seconds!
h: Auction for 1×Human Head ended with no bids.
h: VotedMr5pazm is auctioning 32×Diamond for $3000.
/auc

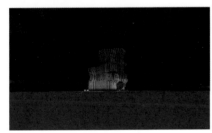

This is a very cool and well-done Factions base that's actually fairly defensible because of its many top layers and the fact that it's on a small island.

- When joining a faction, ask in the chat for a group. Usually someone will reply, and just go ahead and join their faction. You can always leave if you don't like it, and you can't really know if a faction is good or not without trying. Asking specific factions to join is pretty tough and doesn't often result in getting a faction's attention (you can try if you like, but if you don't get a response, don't be a pest). A good faction will have guidelines and some rules but won't be too strict, will have mostly active players, and will allow you to become a part of the group without going through a lot of hazing or tests. If a faction seems like too much trouble, just quit and get a new one!

NOTE: DO NOT join factions, take their things, and then leave. They will tell people, you will get killed, and you will probably get banned. Not to mention no other faction will take you in. Just don't do it. It won't ever go well.

· Attacking factions is called raiding, and though you can't break any blocks in a faction's claimed land the regular ways (hitting them with tools), you CAN do it with other methods. Specifically, you can drop TNT on their buildings.

· Teleporting is important. Many minigames (especially long-form) have the ability to use typed commands to teleport, but in few is it as important as factions. In most Factions servers, there will be specific commands that allow you to teleport to other faction members, your faction homebase, the hub, and random spots in the wilderness. All of these are important, as you might guess (even the wilderness, which is excellent when looking for other factions to raid or for unspoiled land to gather resources in).

· **READ THE HELP SECTION/HELP BOOKS FOR YOUR SERVER.** This is key. It's something that you literally can't ignore unless you have an awesome friend that will explain everything to you out loud. Factions is a minigame with a ton of commands and specific rules for each server, and you'll absolutely need to know these to do just about anything in the game.

Note what happens when a faction builds too close to a spawn point.

COMMON FACTIONS SERVER COMMANDS

/tpa USERNAME – Ask another player to teleport to their location on most servers. This is super useful if you're trying to meet up with someone or get back to where they are. But, don't accept /tpa requests from people you don't know unless you're cool with potentially getting straight up killed. People like to do this, especially to newbs.

/claim—Claim a chunk of land for your faction, using one of your faction's power.

/f—Accesses the faction menus. "/f OPTION," where OPTION stands for one of the faction commands will be the way you access specific faction menus and features on most servers. For instance, "/f create" is typically the command to create a new faction.

TIPS FOR PROS:

- Learn different styles of TNT cannons and get seriously good at them. You'll always be valuable to a faction if you do this.

- Attack any base that hasn't claimed its own land in the Nether by getting the coordinates for the base in the Overworld, dividing by 8, then going to those coordinates in the Nether. You can build a Nether Portal there if the land isn't claimed, and its other side will be inside the enemy base.

This faction decided to build straight up in the air to keep their things safe...

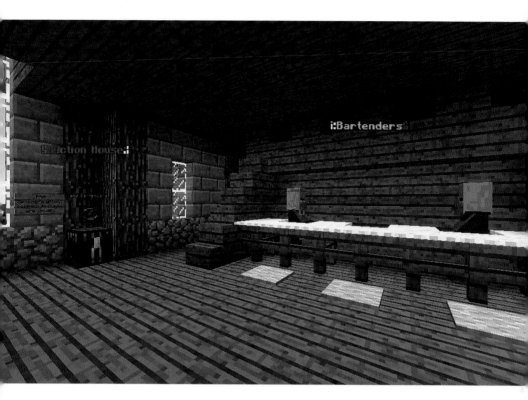

...but as you can see, it doesn't always work.

- Learn how to build walls in layers, using Water, Sand, slabs of different kinds, Fences, Cactus, and Cobblestone to make an intensely good base. Don't bother with Obsidian. It's too costly: work on keeping openings unavailable and keep TNT cannons from being able to work.

MineZ and MineZ 2

Basic idea: *The Walking Dead,* or any "zombies take over the world" post-apocalyptic thing, but in Minecraft and with you as a character.

Number of players: Any amount, just depends on the server. Usually you don't see more than five or six in a session of playing.

How long does it take: Infinite. Another one that goes until the server resets or shuts down.

How hard is it: Not that bad when you haven't attracted Zombies. When you have, look out. The difficulty just compounds. Try to be geared up and know the areas as quick as possible, or death will come fast.

Where can it be found: There are a lot of servers online that do a version of the zombies-in-Minecraft thing, and you can also get the game style in a single-player version with mods. However, the best place to play the zombie-style minigame online has been and continues to be the awesome Shotbow Network, address us.shotbow.net.

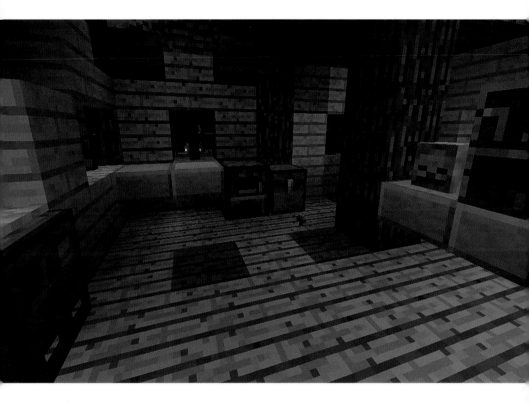

⚙ IMPORTANT FEATURES:

MineZ and most zombie-focused minigames are at their core a variant of survival mode Minecraft, forcing the player to drop randomly onto a map with hostile creatures about. The player has to survive by gathering items, crafting and avoiding being killed, though in this particular case that's a whole lot easier because there are a great many flesh-eating zombies about that don't care if the sun is out or not (like normal Minecraft Zombies do).

In the case of MineZ, Crafting Dead, and most other Zombie-based minigames, however, the map you're placed into is created to be like a real-world zombie-infested landscape, complete with towns, new weapons like guns, and many more "realistic" touches such as bleeding from injuries and having to worry about how much sound you're making.

Basic Strategy for Winning: MineZ is another deeply complex game with a lot to it, but what makes it different from every other minigame, including the other long-form games in this chapter, is that it has more of a narrative to it than other Minecraft styles.

The maps you're playing on when you play online (especially on Shotbow) are very specifically designed, and as you move across them, you'll find yourself encountering a wide range of locations, creatures, items, and even biomes that the map and mod designers have put together for you.

MineZ has a lot of rules and features, which you can read about before entering.

Because of this, it's highly advised to keep up with the state of the game on the server's website, documentation, forums, and wherever else they post about the variant of zombie Minecraft you're playing.

General tips for zombie-based Minecraft:

· This game is about the long haul, not the immediate, so avoid dying at all costs. You will lose your gear and have to start over again if you die on almost every server, so just don't risk it if possible.

A MineZ town. Towns are very important because they have the most resources.

- Chests are the key to this game. Chests with a few items randomly spawn across the map, especially in rooms in houses and buildings in towns. You very much need to find as many of these as you can to get anywhere in this game, and looting these Chests is one of the main focuses of this minigame. You'll get guns, ammo, bandages, water, and every other item in the game, all of which are super useful and necessary. Chests will respawn after a while, but not always in the same exact square and rarely with the same items.

- Blocks don't break according to the same rules as regular Minecraft on some servers. Be aware of what you can and can't manipulate when it comes to the server you're playing on.

- These aren't specifically PVP minigames, but other players can kill you, and you can kill them. You can try to team up with other players in zombie minigames, but just know that they do have the option to attack you at any point. It is not a kind or fair world out there, and it's up to you whether you want to trust other players or not. Don't say we didn't warn you if you get murdered by a greedy player.

Other players in MineZ might be helpful and friendly...but they also might not.

- Damage is not as easily taken or healed in this minigame. Zombie-based games almost always have a bleeding system to them, which means that if you take big damage (such as a heavy zombie attack or a hard fall), you'll keep "bleeding" (taking damage) until you heal yourself a bit. There are bandages and some other medical items on most servers that serve this purpose, and they are very, very valuable items that you'll need to stay alive.

· The game is realistic in other ways that really, seriously matter. Particularly, you need to pay attention to when you can be heard or seen and how thirsty and hungry you are. Your player can die from thirst and hunger on most servers, and you'll need to find clean water and food sources to consume or else you'll find your avatar sick and in worse shape than if you had kept starving or dying of thirst. You also can't go running willy-nillly across the countryside punching zombies with no fear of reprisal—zombies are very sensitive to their surroundings, especially when loud sounds happen or one of their own is attacked, and if you're noticed by a zombie, you can be sure that it will be chasing after you hard for a long while until you're able to get away. Avoid this by being careful, quiet, and thoughtful when you move.

Prison

Basic idea: Play as a prisoner in a working prison with active dangerous zones, building your gear and level from working in the mines and other work locations, and using that gear to defeat other players and even (if available) the guards.

Number of players: Depends on the server, but can be up to a few hundred inmates at a time.

How long does it take: As long as you want to play.

How hard is it: One of the easiest to play. Not much you do is that complicated in terms of the work, but like all long-term minigames, there are ways to gain resources and go up levels faster.

Where can it be found: Infinity servers. This is a big one. Examples include fadecloud.com, mc.arkhamnetwork.org, play.gotpvp.com, play.guildcraft.com, mc.desiredcraft.net, mc-central.net, ubermc.net, and so very many more it's bonkers. This minigame is doing well.

⚙ IMPORTANT FEATURES:

Like the name says, the idea here is that you are in prison, but here's the twist: it's fun! You begin as a prisoner in the lowest ranked "cell block" (often Block D, but it can vary), and you work to earn money, which you then use to move up to higher ranked cell blocks. Eventually, you can earn enough money to gain freedom, at which point you can either lord your wealth over the newbs or (on many servers) become a guard, and eventually even the warden of the prison.

Basic Strategy for Winning: In order to earn money you must collect resources within your cell block to sell at special areas of the map. This is generally done by mining, cutting down trees for Wood, fishing and/or other regular resource collection activities. There will be specific areas in your cell block to gather each resource, and these areas tend to reset every so often so that there are more delicious resources to acquire. You'll usually start off with some tools to allow you to get these needed resources, though on some Prison servers you will have to purchase replacements at a shop.

Players enter and leave the PVP zone on a Prisons server.

Here's where things get tricky: you can't just move around the whole prison as you like. While PVP isn't allowed within your cell block or in designated safe zones, the areas between cell blocks and sometimes even between the selling areas/shops/resource areas are free game as spaces for other prisoners to attack you and take your items. Additionally, you will need to make sure you are not performing any behavior that a guard could get you in trouble for, such as owning a weapon or hanging out in a cell block above your rank.

As they say about the real clink, keep your head down and do your work, and you'll survive. Of course, it can be a lot of fun to be the bad seed in the prison...

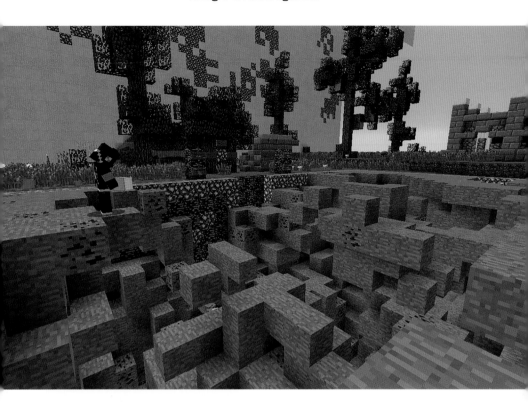

The entrance to Prisons on a Minecraft server.

💡 TIPS FOR PROS:

· Learn what you're best at mining, and do that the most. Mine fast, turn items into things that will help you as fast as you can.

· PVP isn't all that great. It can be very good if you win, but you risk a lot to lose at it. For the most part, run through the PVP areas as fast as possible.

Cops and Robbers

Basic idea: Players play more of a "real prison" game than Prison, where each player has their own cell and has to get up, work, go to sleep and otherwise move about the prison at the command of the guards. Prisoners are trying to reach escapes without dying, and guards are trying to keep them from doing so.

Number of players: Very much depends on who is online, but not more than 24 at a time usually.

How long does it take: Depends on you! The server will keep running, it just depends on you how long it takes to escape, and whether you go back for another term, become a guard, or call it quits.

How hard is it: Pretty hard to escape, easier to be a guard.

Where can it be found: Powercraft.me:25565, playgb.net

This is actually one of the secret escape tunnels from a Cops and Robbers map. Note the need for Parkour skills (or to build a bridge across).

⚙ IMPORTANT FEATURES:

Similar to Prison, Cops & Robbers also puts you in a prison as either a guard or a prisoner, but instead of having the goal of purchasing your freedom, you are attempting to escape the prison without the guard knowing and/or killing you.

As opposed to Prison's shared cell blocks, in Cops & Robbers prisoners will usually have their very own individual cell. Each day, you will wake up and have to move around the prison on a schedule, performing tasks under the watch of the guards. If a guard asks you to do anything, you must comply immediately or risk punishment (such as losing items or being moved to a stronger cell or even being killed).

The prison in Cops and Robbers has many areas you'll become quite familiar with during your stint.

Basic Strategy for Winning: There will be quite a few less guards than prisoners (maybe even just one guard), so the idea is that the guards can't watch everything all the time. Prisoners need to take advantage of any time they can sneak away or do something against the rules (like building weapons or digging escape tunnels) in order to work on escaping.

Winning is slightly different from server to server, but usually the prisoners win if they escape, and the guards win if no one or not enough prisoners have escaped after a certain amount of time.

The "mess hall" where prisoners eat.

💡 TIPS FOR PROS:

- Talk to other players to figure out where the escapes are, or look them up online. If you want to be more realistic about it, look for them yourself, but it can take a really long, frustrating time.

- Pay attention to where the guards are. Act as good as you can when you think you're being watched. Make them think you are bad at this. Not a threat. Make your moves when you know they can't see you.

- Become a guard! If you can get to the point where they'll let you play as a guard, do it. It's a lot of fun!

Creative
Minigames

Now for something completely different, this chapter is all about an entirely unique genre of minigames that touches on that other great part of Minecraft that we don't often see in competitive play: being imaginative and creating something with blocks.

Creative games allow players to let loose their imaginations and create with blocks, but still compete and have limits, such as a timer or having to draw/build a very specific thing.

These games are excellent both for those who are already master creators, as well as those looking to boost their skill levels in the creation side of the game. They're a bit stressful, but incredibly rewarding, and we promise you: you won't be the worst one in the match. Give them a try, and free your inner Minecraft artist.

Champion Builder

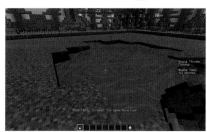

A player works on a build for the word "Fishing."

Basic idea: Use creative mode to create a build based on a word in four minutes. Players vote on their favorite build at the end (without knowing whose it is), and the top voted build wins

Number of players: ~12

How long does it take: About 6 minutes with the voting

How hard is it: Depends on how good you are at building, but pretty hard because of the time limit

Where can it be found: mc-central.net, other servers under various names

⚙ IMPORTANT FEATURES:

In regular Minecraft, building is one of the most important parts of the game. You don't have to build too much or too often in minigames, and you very rarely ever get creative mode access to all the different awesome blocks and items in the game, so generally builds in minigames aren't too creative or impressive.

But not in Champion Builders! Champion Builders is a game all about showing off your imaginative abilities by creating something very fast using all of the blocks in Minecraft. In particular, you have four minutes to create your idea of whatever word the game tells you to. In our examples here, we got the word "knife" the first time and "fishing" the second. You can see from the photos how many different interpretations there were of these two words alone, and that's what this game is all about.

When the four minutes are up, the minigame will cycle through and show everyone's build, and you'll have a chance to vote on each of them (except your own). When all builds have been shown, the game will tally up the votes, and the top player wins a lot of experience!

While we played this on Minecraft Central, this game mode is pretty common around the web, but often comes under different names, so just look out for anything that sounds like it's a building competition to play elsewhere.

Build Theme
Fishing

1st WeAre_Anonymous
2nd 21oscarl
3rd 123jac
4th the_heuronaut
5th ReillyBlocks
6th BielTZK
7th 123emc
8th NinjaGuga

BielTZK

You Earnt 75 Credits
Vote Fairly, It Makes The Game More Fun!
atulations to WeAre_Anonymous for winning Champion

Basic Strategy for Winning: Practicing your building in regular Minecraft, without a timer, is by far the best way to get better at this game. You should be able to think of how to create all sorts of representations of real-world things using Minecraft blocks, like using stacked Fences for flagpoles and Wool for the flag, or using Cobwebs to represent string or ropes. You can also try timing yourself and giving yourself random subjects to build in creative mode, where you won't have the pressure of having other people see your work, and you can try again if you don't like what you did. Just keep practicing, and you'll definitely get better! In fact, this game is actually a great way to improve your build skills overall for regular Minecraft as well (funny how it works both ways).

💡 TIPS FOR PROS:

· KEEP IT SIMPLE. The worst thing you can do is to come up with an idea that is too complex for the four minutes. Do the easiest, best-looking thing you can think of, and if you have extra time, add more detail.

· Be very creative with what blocks you use. Blocks don't have to represent what they actually are: you can use them to represent something else entirely (like using Glass for eyes or Wool for making an animal, for example). People will understand what you were trying to do more often than you'd think.

Draw My Thing

The word for this match ended up being "Kiss," but nobody got it (not everyone is awesome at this game).

Basic idea: Players take turns quickly drawing a representation of a word on a flat screen in front of other players, who try and guess the word for points.

Number of players: ~8

How long does it take: About 10 minutes

How hard is it: Depends on how creative/ good at pixel drawing people are, but guessing is easier than drawing

Where can it be found: us.mineplex.com

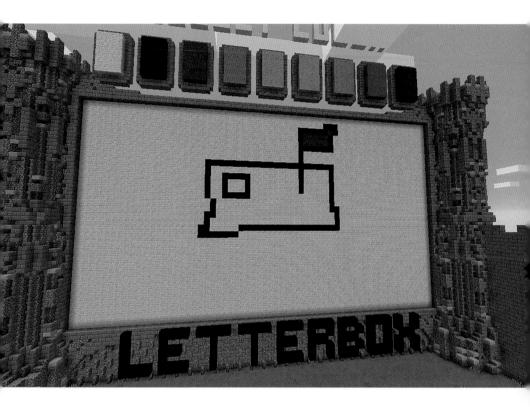

Some players, though, are pretty darn good at drawing quickly!

⚙ IMPORTANT FEATURES:

If you've ever played Pictionary, you understand this game. Draw My Thing is a game where one player is given a word that the other players can't see, and that player tries to draw it on a giant, flat board with different colored blocks. You can only use different colors of Wool, no items, and you have very little time to draw each word. If another player can guess it, you both get points.

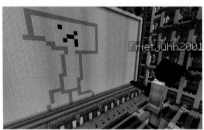

Can you guess what this little guy is?

Basic Strategy for Winning: Like the other games in this chapter, getting good at this game is really just about being creative and practicing drawing things fast. People who are good at pixel art should be awesome at this, as will people who are good at Pictionary. You can practice on your own, trying to draw subjects very fast with blocks in creative mode, to get better. On the guesser's side, try to pay attention to the parts of the drawing that the player is focusing on the most, and guess as many things as you can think of. You never know when that one thought you had that you were sure wasn't it ends up being the answer.

Players stand watching and guessing.

💡 TIPS FOR PROS:

· Again, KEEP IT SIMPLE when drawing. You only have so much time, and in this case you don't win points for it looking awesome. You just want the other players to guess it, so just draw whatever the least you need to is for that to happen.

· DON'T cheat and just write the word. People will get mad and kick you out, and you might get further punished by the server. Everyone knows they can do this, but it ruins the game.

Pixel Painters

Pixel Painting is pretty difficult—some people (like your writer here) can really only do very basic shapes.

Basic idea: Players have a limited amount of time to draw their idea of a word on a blank floor with colored blocks, and after the time is up, everyone votes on the best ones.

Number of players: ~8

How long does it take: About 6 minutes

How hard is it: We'll sound like a broken record here, but again, it just depends on how good you are at drawing with blocks. For us it's pretty hard, but some talented and artistic players are very, very good at this game.

Where can it be found: mc.hypixel.net, other variations under different names around the Internet

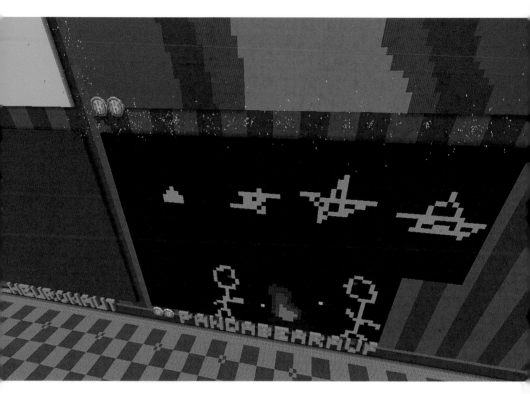

⚙ IMPORTANT FEATURES:

Pixel Painters is almost exactly like Champion Builders, except instead of doing 3D builds, you create flat 2D pictures out of colored Wool blocks. Otherwise it works the same way: you have just a few minutes to draw your idea of the word the game gives you, and when the time is up, everyone gets to see all of the drawings and votes on their favorites.

The instructions for this minigame are pretty simple, and very visibly posted.

Basic Strategy for Winning: You really just can't get better at this without practice! Even more so than Champion Builders, you really have to sit down and try drawing things with blocks in creative mode to raise your skill level at this minigame, because pixel painting just isn't something most players do in regular play. It is, however, its own subgenre of Minecraft creating, so if you like it, keep doing it in regular creative mode! Some of the best builds we've ever seen were pixel paintings, like the incredible Mona Lisa or the massive Notch's face that you can find online (try Googling those terms + Minecraft build and just see how impressive these things are). Give pixel painting a try! Maybe you'll become the next Minecasso.

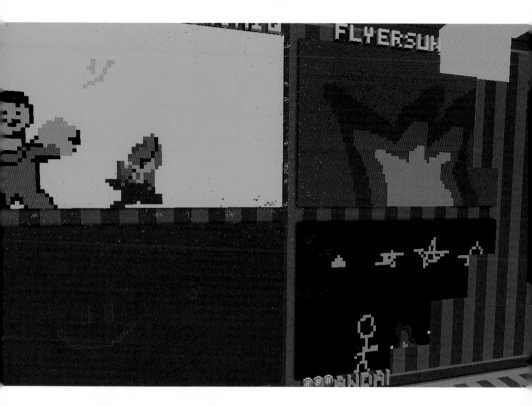

The word for this match was "Bacon."

⚑ TIPS FOR PROS:

· Can you guess it? KEEP IT SIMPLE. You've got almost no time here, so just do the easiest picture you can while still making it look like the word it gives you. Add flair at the end, when you've got something acceptable already made, and you'll do much better than if you try to make it perfect and complex from the get-go.

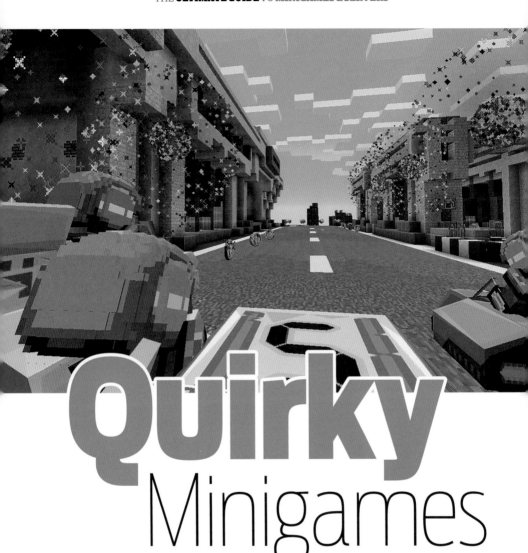

Quirky Minigames

Some of the best minigames that are out there in the wide world of Minecraft don't really fit a specific category—that's how creative and inventive they are! Players love the goofiness and lighthearted nature of this style of minigames, and in fact, many of these kind of games, that include everything from Mario Kart-style racers to an awesome hide n' seek variant, are among the most popular games on their server. Here's a selection of some of our very favorite quirky minigames, and where you can go play them for yourself right now.

Playing TURBO KART RACERS on MC.HYPIXEL.NET

Turbo Kart Racers

Basic idea: A racing game with power-ups and weapons, very much like Mario Kart

Number of players: Up to 12

How long does it take: ~5 minutes

How hard is it: Harder than it looks! But mostly it's just the car controls that take getting used to; anyone should be able to play this one

Where can it be found: mc.hypixel.net

⚙ IMPORTANT FEATURES:

· 5 different maps to race on, mostly based on Mario Kart levels

· Kart parts that can be earned through playing, including new kart bodies, particle trails and a variety of fun horns

· A lobby before each match where you can test out how the controls work

· A wide variety of weapons including (but not limited to, as some are added all the time): bananas, missiles, lightning, fireballs, snowballs, and TNT

· Boosts and jumps along the tracks, as well as dangerous sections that you have to avoid to stay ahead!

The always-fun Hypixel server is where you'll find this little gem of a minigame. One of the very best racer games out there, it uses a mod system that auto-loads when you get in the hub for Turbo Kart Racers to add go-karts, all sorts of weapons, new skins for your player, and more to Minecraft. Put all of that into a racetrack and add in a system that keeps track of how many laps each player has made and who is in front of who, and you've got all you need for an awesome competitive racing game!

Basic Strategy for Winning: Like in real Mario Kart, the keys to winning this game are all about avoiding obstacles, driving efficiently and collecting weapons to use at just the right time.

When it comes to the driving, getting used to the controls is really the best thing you can do. It's really easy to over-turn, because the mod that puts the karts in the game doesn't turn smoothly, but instead will turn a pre-set amount each time you tap left or right on your keys. Because of this, what you want to do is not to hold the keys down to turn, but instead to tap them just enough times that you're pointed in the right direction. For big turns, tap very rapidly, but try not to tap even one time too many, or you'll turn too far.

🔥 HOT TIP

Tapping to turn to just the right direction is also important for trying to get out of corners or around obstacles you hit. When this happens, stay calm and try to carefully get yourself out of the corner or away from the obstacle. It's really easy to panic and try to slam keys to get out, but this almost always ends up taking more time than slowly and carefully pulling yourself out of the jam. If you're fast, you can also open up the Minecraft console and type "/stuck" to get out of corners if you can't get yourself out.

TURBO KART RA

Position:
3 GATORBALL13
4 BlueBoyPeck
5 the_heuronau
6 shenry024
...

Item:
?????????

Map:
Jungle Rush

www.hypixel.net

Position: #5 – Lap: 2 – Progress: 88.6% – Coins: 33
Green Missile

coins) Picked up a coin!
shoot a fireball!

68

Standard driving-game strategies also apply in this minigame and will help out a lot. For instance, make sure you get a good start when the game goes, and always try to take the shortest possible route across the track. Hug corners and avoid going out of your way to get items or look at things: instead, go straight through the track as fast as possible.

Weapons-wise, the golden rule is to make sure you use each weapon before you run into the next place to pick them up, but don't waste them. If you have a good weapon, but no one is around, hold onto it. If you see someone and you're armed, go ahead and use it!

💡 TIPS FOR PRO KARTING:

- Drop bananas around sharp corners or where people land for a jump. These are very hard to avoid and will very likely slow your opponents. Another good idea is to drop bananas when you know someone is right behind you, or right at the finish line. Both of these will not only help you win, but they're also pretty funny to see.

- The "sneak" or "crouch" button is used in Turbo Kart Racers as a drifting button. This gives you better control when going around corners and can make a big difference if you get good at using it.

- Turning your kart charges up a boost that you can use to get a slight jump on enemies.

- Fire the Red Missile when very close to an enemy for best results.

- You can actually turn around while moving forward (turn your player around in your kart) and fire weapons in any direction, including backwards.

Block Hunt / Hide 'n Seek

Basic idea: Players disguised as various blocks and items hide from seekers that are trying to kill them.

Number of players: Up to ~24

How long does it take: About 3 minutes a round

How hard is it: Very easy to learn, but sometimes very hard to find the hiders!

Where can it be found: us.mineplex.com, play.hivemc.com, mc.comugamers.com

⚙ IMPORTANT FEATURES:

Players that are on the "hiders" team have avatars that look like various items in Minecraft (such as Anvils, Bookshelves etc.) and they must hide in a map full of items. Players on the "seekers" team run around the map trying to find the hiders by hitting items. When a hider is killed, he joins the seekers team. The hiders win if there are one or more hiders alive when the match timer finishes, and seekers win if they find all the hiders.

Each game starts with the hiders picking the type of block they want to be (some servers assign them randomly), and they are then given a minute or so to hide on a pre-made map.

Screenshot: Minecraft® ™ & © 2009–2016 Mojang/Notch

Seekers have a certain amount of time to find and kill all of the hiding blocks, and they are outfitted with armor and weapons. Hiders sometimes have a weak weapon, and on some servers you can gradually upgrade your weapon by doing things like making noise or hitting a seeker. If the hiders make it through the time limit without dying, they win!

Basic Strategy for Winning: These maps are usually made so that there are a lot more of the type of block you choose to be, so it's a good idea to find a place with a bunch of blocks that look like you and hide by them. Some servers actually allow you to select a block in the map and become it, which makes this easier. You want to make

the hiding look natural, so that the seeker will just run past, but don't worry about lining up perfectly with the other blocks—the minigame will make it so that your block will appear to be lined up and perfectly still as long as you put yourself squarely on a block and aren't walking, meaning you can look around all you like.

💡 TIPS FOR PROS:

- Many of these maps have "holes" in piles of the same kind of block where it looks like another block of the same kind could go. These are good spots to hide, though some players might know the map so well that they recognize where the hole should be.

- If you know a map well, you can find places where you can jump up to hard to access areas of the map. These are some of the best hiding spots because most players won't know how to get there, but it will also be pretty obvious if someone does make it up that you are hiding there because you won't look like any of the surrounding blocks.

- As a seeker, be hitting constantly as you move around, and never stay in one place for long. Pay attention to when the sound for you hitting a character happens, and also for when you get hit yourself. If either of these happens, you know a hider is close by.

- If you're on one of the servers that lets you upgrade weapons and earn points by hitting seekers as a hider, be sneaky about it and do it as much as you can. You'll usually earn coins or other points for the server as a whole if you're able to do this a lot in a match, and it can really frustrate your seekers. It's best to use ranged weapons to do this, and to only shoot at the seekers when they aren't looking your direction. NOTE: your Arrows will stick in whatever they hit, and a smart player can see what direction they came from by where they point, so be careful when and where you shoot!

TNT Run

Basic idea: Blocks fall out from an arena after a player runs over them, last player alive wins!

Number of players: Many! Just depends on the server, but sometimes there are as many as 40+

How long does it take: ~2 minutes

Where can it be found: mc.hypixel.net, Banana (212.224.87.118:19132)

⚙ IMPORTANT FEATURES:

TNT Run has been around for a long time, and it involves running around in an arena on a flat surface that will fall out underneath you as you go. That means that if you step on a block, you better move quickly because soon that block will drop and you'll fall to the next layer below.

Some players get a little confused about TNT Run's name, as there are no explosions in this minigame. The reason the game is named after the 'splodiest block in Minecraft is that there is a block of TNT under each block that makes up the layers of the arena. The game has been specially designed so that walking on the Sand or Gravel blocks that make up the floor of each layer causes the TNT to activate beneath the Sand or Gravel, causing the Sand or Gravel to fall, though without causing an explosion. Essentially it's just a trick to get the game to work, so no need to worry about getting blown up in this minigame. Just worry about where you're going to put your feet next!

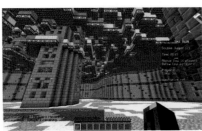

Basic Strategy for Winning: The idea is to keep moving around and create holes in the ground as you move that other players fall into. Since these players are creating more holes themselves, you'll need to keep on your toes and plan out where you run, deftly jumping any holes that you can't run around.

When you fall to the next layer, you'll do the same thing there, and the player that is able to keep from falling through the final layer of the arena and into the darkness below is the winner.

💡 TIPS FOR PROS:

· The best strategy is a combination of long

bursts of movement across the whole map combined with a few seconds of moving more slowly in an area to see where other people are and to let people knock each other out.

· WATCH YOUR FEET. The easiest way to lose at this game is to think there is a block where there is none and to just run right over it.

· At the beginning, focus on staying on blocks and removing as many as you can. Don't go after other players unless it's very easy to.

attack when one is isolated, and avoid big bunches of players (it's harder to know what blocks will fall).

· In the later game, focus on where the other players are. Be opportunistic and

Block Party

Basic idea: Players have to stand on blocks of an indicated color or fall to their doom.

Number of players: Up to 20

How long does it take: Depends, but usually less than 5 minutes for a whole game

How hard is it: Very easy to learn, but winning a game can take a lot of tries

Where can it be found: play.hivemc.com

⚙ IMPORTANT FEATURES:

Players are in an arena with a floor made of colored Wool that changes its pattern every round. Music will play for few seconds at the beginning of the round, and then a color will be indicated at the top of the screen. Players need to run to stand on that color of block before the (very fast) timer counts down. When the timer hits zero, all the other blocks in the arena except those of that color will disappear, and players that didn't get to safety in time will fall and be out of the game. The game keeps going until there's just one person left.

Screenshot: Minecraft® ™ & © 2009–2016 Mojang/Notch

Each round, the time you have to get to your color will be shorter, meaning it gets harder and more frantic with each turn. Also, there are some sweet power-ups in some versions of this game, which can help you quite a lot!

Basic Strategy for Winning: The best idea is to try and find areas with the most colors in a bunch and stand between them. This way you'll need way less time to run to one of the blocks. That is, if the bunch of colors you've stood by contains the one you need!

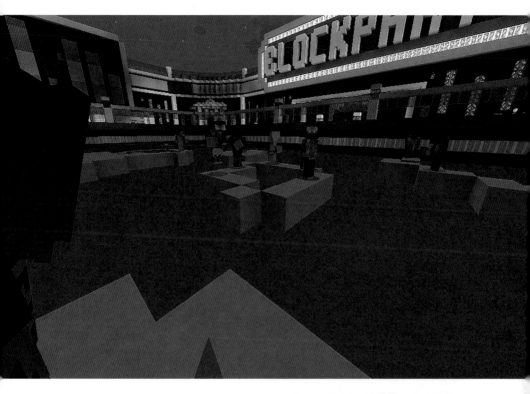

💡 TIPS FOR PROS:

- It can help to be already in "run" mode (double tapping forward) when the color indicator goes off, so that you're already at top speed.

- Jumping while running makes you move a bit faster but has to be done just right to keep up the rhythm, so if you're good at this technique, try it out (otherwise it might be more trouble than it's worth).

- Try to get a good view of all or most of the arena floor before the color indicator comes up, so you have a good idea of where to run. Most of the floors have patterns, so you should be able to know what the rest of the ground looks like just by looking in one area (this is not always the case).

- Practice to get better! But, realize that this game can sometimes be lost and there's not much you can do about it, because you only have so much time. It's more about having fun and watching people fall to their doom than it is about skill, so just enjoy yourself!

183

Server Spotlight

Servers are sources of endless cool stuff to look at, like this awesome castle.

Over the course of showing you all these sweet, sweet minigames, we've talked a good bit about the different servers you can find them on, and given you some addresses to check out, but we haven't gotten that much into the makeup of these servers.

Minecraft is a lucky game, where the format itself allows for people to create incredible, unique virtual places for people all over the world to come visit, hang out and (of course) play minigames anytime they like. A lot of these computer-based destinations are pretty cool, but there are some out there that are just stunning, both in the way they've been visually designed and in the scope of features and activities they make available to players (for free!).

Server Spotlight

This is Skygrid on Lichcraft, one of the cooler Skyblock variants.

Now, new servers go online every day, and the most popular can change pretty quickly, but here's a quick tour of some of our current favorites and some of the classic locations in the vast ocean of online Minecraft servers. We've included a list of the currently available minigames on each of these (note that available games do change pretty regularly on servers, so this is more of a snapshot than a directory), as well as some shots of the hubs on these servers, which always feature some deeply impressive architecture.

We think you'll dig all of these servers, and you absolutely should take a few minutes and check each of them out yourself. You'll find them full of friendly folks, awesome features, and enough minigames to satisfy you for one wild, blocky lifetime.

Arkham Network

A Grand Theft Auto remake on the Arkham Network.

Address: mc.arkhamnetwork.org

The Arkham Network consistently comes up in "best of" lists for Minecraft servers because it is one of the most well-oiled and fun competitive servers that exist today. You'll almost always find thousands of other players on the Arkham Network no matter when you log in, and it features a semi-rotating crop of the most popular styles of play and minigames, adding more as they are invented. Like most good servers it features a creative zone, too, though it is not nearly as popular on this server as the minigames and PVP sections.

CURRENT MINIGAMES SNAPSHOT:

- Skyblock
- Factions (regular and hardcore)
- Prison
- Skywars
- Skygrid
- Epic Kit PVP
- GTA
- TNT Wars
- Towny
- Survival Games

The Hive

The Hive has some very cool unique minigames like Cowboys and Indians.

Address: play.hivemc.com

The Hive is always abuzz with players, being another of the bigger top Minecraft servers around. It's one with a deep ranking/money/rewards system, and the games are well-organized, well-kept up, and well-populated pretty much all around. It has an equal amount of classic games (Splegg, Survival, Blockparty, Skywars) and more rare games (Cowboys and Indians, Trouble in Mineville, The Lab), which combines with its excellence in production (as in stuff doesn't break much, looks great and is easy to use) and a very heavy population to be one of the best experiences you can have on a Minecraft server.

CURRENT MINIGAMES SNAPSHOT:

- Survival Games
- Trouble in Mineville
- The Herobine
- Hide and Seek
- Splegg
- One in the Chamber
- Cowboys and Indians
- Blockparty
- Survival Games: Heroes
- Death Run
- The Lab
- Drawit
- Skywars

TURBO KART RA

Position:
5 superAidanbe
6 epicgamer133
7 the_heuronau

Item:
Fire Flower

Map:
Canyon

www.hypixel.net

Position: #7 - Lap: 2 - Progress: 57.5% - Coins: 16

lBoop has taken the lead!

Hypixel

Hypixel is perhaps the most beloved and busy server of all!

Address: mc.hypixel.net

The great Hypixel's personally hosted server, hypixel.net is another quality competition/PvP server and one of the more frequented servers online. Since it is run by one of the bigger personalities in the game, you can sometimes find "celeb" players here as well as a very well-updated list of minigames and competitions. Plus, because of the quality of folks involved, everything in it runs very smoothly and looks incredible! This is another one with a lot of unique games, mostly created by the spectacularly creative Hypixel team, and it's also the only place to really play The Walls (because, again, it was made by these dudes).

CURRENT MINIGAMES SNAPSHOT:

· The Walls (regular, mega, and crazy)
· Blitz Survival Games
· Skywars
· Turbo Kart Racers
· UHC (Regular and Champions)
· Warlords
· Cops and Crims
· Arena Brawl
· ARCADE!
· Build Battle
· Galaxy Wars
· Hole in the Wall
· The Blocking Dead
· Farm Hunt
· Creeper Attack
· Party Games
· Ender Spleef
· Bounty Hunters
· Dragon Wars

· TNT Games
· QuakeCraft
· VampireZ
· Paintball Warfare
· Pixel Painters
· Build Battle

Lichcraft

The server selection hub for Lichcraft uses mobs to choose which game you want to play.

Address: us.lichcraft.com

Consistently ranked among the top servers online, Lichcraft is similar to Hypixel and the Arkham Network but with a few different games to play. This is another server with a very well-run peripheral portion, meaning the ranks, currency, kits, and rewards are super deep and complex, and the whole interface to interact with the server is solid and easy to use. Lichcraft tends to stick to the most popular minigames, but does them super well, so if what you're looking for is some classic/popular minigame action as good as it can get, this is a server you'll dig.

Type /leave to quit the game!
the_heuronaut joined team red.
L10nelMessi joined team blue.

CURRENT MINIGAMES SNAPSHOT:

- Skyblock
- Factions (regular and hardcore)
- Survivor (regular and hardcore)
- Prison
- Duels
- Skygrid
- Prophunt
- Walls
- Skywars
- CTF
- Bomb

MindCrack

Address: us.playmindcrack.com

There are actually two MindCrack servers (at least): the private one played on by Guude and the other members of the famous MindCrack Network, which is the subject of many incredibly popular YouTube video series, and then the public MindCrack server, which is this one. While it's pretty hard to get an invitation to the private MindCrack server, the public server is an example of the highest quality server that a regular Minecrafter can get on. Not only can you tour the maps from old seasons of the MindCrack video series, literally stepping virtual foot where some of the best Crafters in the world once built, you can also play the minigames created by this untouchably talented crew of builders and YouTubers. Many of the great Redstone engineer SethBling's minigame creations are tested first on this server, such as the wild and explosive Missile Wars game he created with Cubehamster, and indeed most of the minigames found here are not seen elsewhere. Along with 2b2t, Hypixel, and WesterosCraft, the MindCrack server sits among online royalty when it comes to public servers.

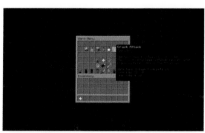

CURRENT MINIGAMES SNAPSHOT:
- 9 Lives
- MindCrack Survival Games
- Splat
- Missile Wars
- UHC
- Crack Attack

Minecade

Like most big servers, Minecade has an extensive features system, including different player classes.

Address: mineca.de

You can't go wrong at the Minecade, whether you're looking for some classic play, something you won't find elsewhere or a really nicely set up ranking and rewards system. It's a pretty server, built with thought and skill, and they live up to their name by making it easy to pop in a play a few rounds of a fun game, just like an arcade. A few of these games are pretty unique to the server, like Run from the Beast and Villager Defense, and you should absolutely check them out because they're as fun as shooting Creepers in a pit (One where they can't get to you. 'Splode, little green dudes. 'Splode.).

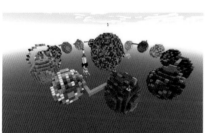

CURRENT MINIGAMES SNAPSHOT:

- Run from the Beast
- Sky Wars
- Super Craft Brothers
- The Walls
- Farm Frenzy
- Santa's Workshop
- Survival Games
- Villager Defense

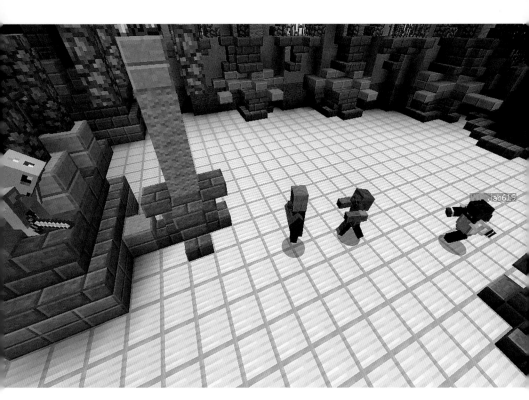

Minecraft Central

The initial spawn hub for Minecraft Central is simple but easy to use, and their minigames are top-notch.

Address: mc-central.net

Minecraft Central is a combination of the competitive style of server and the creative style. It features both, and both see a pretty good amount of use. Here you see the creative section, which is set up in a grid like many others. It's somewhat uncommon for a server to have active communities on both sides of the server spectrum, which makes MC Central one of the more well-rounded servers that actually has a big, active community. Make sure you check out the Arcade section especially, as it's one of the prime examples of why an Arcade area with a lot of party-style games is just plain awesome fun.

Server Spotlight

CURRENT MINIGAMES SNAPSHOT:
- Skyblock
- KitPVP
- Prison
- Survival
- Factions
- Skywars (regular and teams)
- Champion Builder
- UHC
- CTF
- Arcade!

Mineplex

Another server with a whole bunch of rare games that you don't see often, Mineplex is among the best and most busy servers.

Address: us.mineplex.com

A top minigame server, Mineplex typically is one of the very busiest servers, often with over 10,000 players online at a time. In fact, at the time of this writing it has a whopping 13,354 Minecrafters on it enjoying the entertainment it has to offer. Mineplex is professionally run, with server hosts that really pay attention to the desires of their virtual denizens and who are constantly adding new features, tweaking things to be better and throwing special events just to make things that much more fun. Maybe one of the best features on any server is Mineplex's Arcade, where they mix up a ton of fun minigames that play one after the other, so you only have to load into a lobby once.

CURRENT MINIGAMES SNAPSHOT:

- Draw My Thing
- Castle Siege
- Block Hunt
- Super Smash Mobs
- Mine-Strike
- Master Builders
- ARCADE!
- Wither Assault
- Micro Battle
- Snake
- Death Tag
- Super Paintball
- One in the Quiver
- Sheep Quest
- Dragons
- Dragon Escape
- Turf Wars
- Runner
- Super Spleef
- Sneaky Assassins
- Bacon Brawl
- Bomb Lobbers
- The Bridges
- Survival Games
- Ultra Hardcore
- Wizards
- Skywars
- Dominate
- Team Deathmatch
- Clans

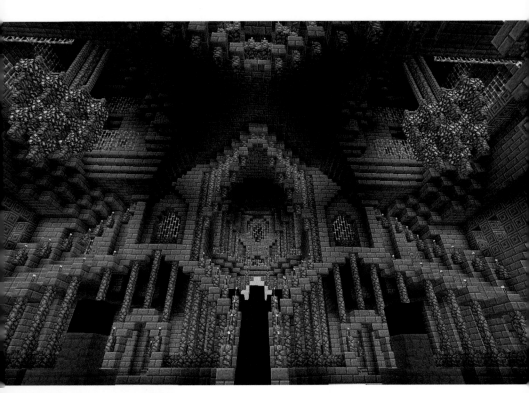

The Shotbow Network

Address: us.shotbow.net

Most servers, including The Shotbow Network, are actually collections of servers with a central hub. When you login to the hub, it gives you portals to various game types, and when you run through these portals, you actually are transferred to a server that hosts that particular game type for the parent server. Like Lichcraft and the Arkham Network, The Shotbow Network is one of the most extensive collections of unique minigame, PVP, and competition servers. For instance, you can find games like Light Bikes, a Tron- style fight to the death on a grid with motorcycles that leave a wall behind them, as well as Flappy Bird and Crafting Mama, games based on other popular video games but recreated in Minecraft.

CURRENT MINIGAMES SNAPSHOT:
- Annihilation
- MineZ/Minez2
- Smash
- Wasted
- Rogue
- Assault
- Ghost Craft
- Ubion Creative
- Slaughter
- Death by Void
- Crafty Bomber
- Light Bikes
- Flappy Chick
- Crafting Mama
- Hidden in Plain Sight

Welcome to BisectHosting

WE ARE DEDICATED TO MAKE YOUR MINECRAFT SERVER HOSTING EXPERIENCE AS
EASY AND AFFORDABLE AS IT CAN POSSIBLY BE.

SEE FEATURES   **SEE PLANS**

Sales C

Daniel
Welco
questi
choosi

Free Unlimited Slots

Free Dedicated IP

Free Modpack Installation

Solid State Drives

Take Control of the Adventure: Host Your Own Server!

If you play Minecraft on the PC, chances are you've thought about how cool it would be to be able to play with your friends on your own server. While you can always play a LAN game with friends, or get on a public server, if you want to play on a private world with people online, you either have to have your own dedicated server running or know someone who does.

Setting up a server is totally do-able, but it takes a lot of time and effort, and a lot can go wrong. Try and add something like mods or big maps in there, and you'll quickly run into trouble. Typically people need an entire computer dedicated to running the server, plus a lot of expertise on server upkeep.

That's where server hosting sites come in: you just pay them a monthly fee, and they do the work and set up a server for you. There are a ton of options out there when it comes to pricing and what you get for your dollar, including hosts that will add mods for you, servers that allow many people to join at once and much more.

It's not something all players will want to do, but there really is something special about getting your own permanent game going with friends from all over the world, so if that sounds fun, definitely check out server hosting sites online.